LOGGED ON

For our next generation of innovators: Anna, Claire, Zain, Shayan, Fatima, Bibi, Bano, Drew and Jack

Our hope is that you will follow the words of John Lennon and *"Imagine"*

LOGGED ON

SMART GOVERNMENT SOLUTIONS FROM SOUTH ASIA

Zubair K. Bhatti, Jody Zall Kusek, and Tony Verheijen

 WORLD BANK GROUP

Contents

Foreword

Great leaders have always made use of the technology of their time to communicate in new ways with the people they lead. In the last century, the advent of radio and then television dramatically increased the ability of leaders to communicate to people in their homes and communities. Millions of citizens and subjects could *hear* and then *see* their leaders for the first time.

The authors of *Logged On: Smart Government Solutions from South Asia* describe exciting examples of how the rapid expansion of a 21st-century innovation—mobile technology—is providing a new set of tools to the leaders of today to *interact* with people in new ways and potentially change how government can deliver services, receive feedback, and achieve results.

This book makes a valuable contribution by collecting many examples of innovators using these new technologies in new ways in South Asia and other regions. There are dozens of cases and "good practices" that will serve to inspire others and suggest approaches to solving problems and providing services in new and more efficient and cost-effective ways. For example, the book describes how these technologies are being used to support:

- Proactive calling of citizens to obtain feedback about government services in rural Pakistan
- Monitoring attendance of school teachers and health care workers
- Farmers, with real-time weather and market price alerts in China, India, Malaysia, and Uganda, and more efficient scheduling for crushing sugarcane in Bangladesh
- Early warning of floods in Bangladesh and typhoons in China
- Payment of taxes, booking appointments, registering a vehicle, and obtaining a birth certificate or an application for a government job

- Registration of voters and monitoring of elections
- An emergency messaging system for women and senior citizens to send the individual's location to close relatives and to the police
- Citizen feedback on government performance and areas that need improvement

What makes mobile technology such an important tool to improve governance?

No other technology in history has spread as widely and as rapidly or penetrated as deeply across economic, social, gender, age, and other barriers. Because of the massive infrastructure investment required, fixed phone coverage in the developing world has grown at a snail's pace. In contrast, over the space of a scant decade, the number of mobile subscriptions has grown from just over 2 billion worldwide in 2005 to nearly 7 billion mobile subscribers in 2014—with most of the growth occurring in the developing world (http://www.itu.int/en/ITU-D/Statistics/Documents/facts/ICTFactsFigures2014-e.pdf).

In 2014, with mobile penetration reaching 96 percent worldwide and 90 percent in the developing world, it is nearing the point where there will be a mobile phone in the hands and pockets of almost every individual around the world—in every country, rich and poor, men and women. No other technology has approached the ubiquity of mobile phones or their ability to connect the people of this world.

Furthermore, a mobile phone is more than a phone. Even the most basic phones, generally known as "feature phones," can do more than call another phone. Simple phones can receive and send voice and text messages, respond to both voice and text surveys, provide access to call centers, and receive broadcast messages (robocalls). And even basic phones are increasingly offering more features and functionality, including e-mail and Internet access.

More sophisticated mobile phones—smartphones—are designed to use the Internet, incorporate specialized applications or "apps," and access mobile websites designed for use on mobile devices. These phones may cost more and reach fewer people but offer more and more exciting features and functionality. Their use is growing, as well, with almost a third of people in many developing countries using smartphones and 44 percent having access to the Internet.

Of course, mobile technology is inherently interactive. No other technology has allowed such direct and personal communication between and among individuals. Fundamentally, mobile phones can change the nature of communication. Unlike earlier tools that allowed leaders to *broadcast* information messages, mobile phones allow people to *interact with* their leaders and leaders to *hear from* their citizens and subjects. As this book argues, this two-way communication can dramatically shift the balance of power and open up many new possibilities for communicating messages from leaders and receiving information and feedback from people.

Now, one might conclude that if you run out and sling together an app, government will be transformed and social change will follow. Well, as much as we might wish that, of course, nothing is that simple. So let me close by describing some of the other characteristics illustrated by several of the cases presented here and others drawn from my own experience developing and using mobile tools for public health and safety in Africa, Asia, and Latin and North America.

Goals, Objectives, and Plans

Clearly, having a hammer does not result in a house. As with any tool, one must first decide what is going to be built, have a plan, and assemble the necessary elements. As an organization focuses on its goals and develops plans to achieve them, new technologies can offer new and often more cost-effective ways to achieve them.

Right Data, Right Scale

Ponderous amounts of data have been collected in the name of monitoring the performance of government programs. New technologies also offer exciting opportunities to obtain data.

Technology

In relating his experience in the Punjab, Zubair Bhatti emphasizes how he harnessed "the power of call centers, text messages, and personal calls." Many different tools and technologies are encompassed by the broad term "mobile." In my experience, while new functionality can present great possibilities, the most important tools can be those that have the greatest reach, not necessarily the greatest amount of functionality. And as the book describes, the most effective strategies usually integrate more than one tool—call centers and text messages or text messaging used by individuals to send and receive information that is stored in databases and accessible via web-based portals, dashboards, and other means. A case in point is the multiple digital tools put in place to monitor waste collection in Lahore, from tracking the trucks to capturing citizen complaints via a third-party call center.

Bear in mind as well that we are only at the beginning of the mobile revolution. New technology is emerging, and more features and functions are added to mobile phones every day—from location tracking to digital photography and devices such as glucometers, activity trackers, and other tools that are integrated with mobile phones or are mobile-enabled. It is impossible to predict the future, but phones, calls, messaging, and data will continue to drop in price as they become commoditized—making smartphones and emerging features and data more accessible and affordable. There will be more power-efficient devices that will lower energy costs and allow access to more features in resource-constrained environments. And there will be ever more features and functionality on this dynamic "personal platform."

Privacy and Protection of Individuals

I would like to reinforce a caution that is touched on in this book: the need to respect the privacy and protection of individuals in face of the dizzying pace of development of this new technology. In the rush to use these new mobile tools in new ways, we must be sensitive to the fact that mobile technology allows an entirely unprecedented amount of information to be collected and shared about an individual—including his or her location, contacts, photographs, opinions, health, and financial status. The potential for this information to be used for positive purposes is enormous. The reverse is also true.

Governments, industry, and individuals are only starting to understand and grapple with the protections that are needed to protect the privacy and security of such information. What is possible to do may not always be desirable, and the emerging debate will unfold in country after country and shape how the public and the private sectors collect and use mobile information in the future. The sweeping June 25, 2014, decision of the U.S. Supreme Court protecting digital privacy is a harbinger of the dialogue ahead—with the Chief Justice noting, "Modern cell phones are not just another technological convenience. With all they contain and all they may reveal, they hold for many Americans 'the privacies of life.'"

People

In the final analysis, this is not a book about technology. This is a book about the people who have the passion, use the tools, make the decisions, and make a difference. Leadership is critical. Technology is a tool, not a solution. The vision and courage of current and former leaders, such as Narendra Modi of India, Agnes Binagwaho of Rwanda, and Sri Mulyani Indrawati of Indonesia, are needed to realize its potential.

Technology gives leaders tools to help them address very large, seemingly intractable problems—such as corruption—and other challenges facing 21st-century leaders, such as more accountability for results, demands for better service, more stakeholders, and greater transparency. New mobile technologies are letting governments interact with the public, reinvent services, and collect the data that allow them to monitor performance in real time.

But it is the employees, supervisors, managers, and leaders who will set the goals, decide to obtain feedback, select the data to monitor, review the results, and make decisions about how to respond. And ultimately, it is this new generation of innovators and leaders, at all levels and in all sectors, who will encourage people to engage with their governments through technology and build a new bond of trust between government and the people that government serves.

Pamela Johnson PhD
Co-founder and Chief Health Officer
Voxiva, Inc.

Preface and Acknowledgments

Our interest in writing this book began nearly a decade ago—years before most of the technological innovations we discuss were even imagined by development professionals as future tools in their work. At that time, each of us was working in the field of public management: in Pakistan, in Central and Eastern Europe, and in Washington, DC.

We witnessed firsthand the government reforms being introduced, adopted, and then often discarded in each of our countries. We observed closely—as eager students of public management—the reforms under way in other countries around the world as well. At that time, in many developing countries citizens' voices were unheard and rarely taken seriously by governments. In Pakistan, a military dictator, after booting out a democratically elected government with embarrassing ease, was ruling without any opposition in sight. Barring some token crumbs thrown here and there to placate some restless groups, it was business as usual. Governments always had the final say, dictating the actions they would take and the amount of taxpayers' money they would spend.

In the Western and developed world, New Public Management reforms aimed to overhaul "business as usual." The reforms brought the notion of performance contracts into government, assigning clear responsibility and accountability for service delivery and regulation. New Public Management also initiated efforts to give greater voice to clients, particularly through the creation of "citizens' charters" and other explicit and contestable commitments to delivery standards. Finally, New Public Management pushed government to focus on core services, rather than be involved in everything, from social services to mining and car manufacturing, as had been the case in many countries.

Some of those attempts took hold, especially when it came to getting the state to focus on core services. But it is important to note that the reforms were intended (and designed) for countries where citizens already assumed that essential services, such as education, health services, water, and sanitation, would be delivered when they needed them.

Progress has undoubtedly been made in creating core public services in developing countries, but access and quality remain major challenges. In African countries, problems such as overpopulated schools without teachers or textbooks, medical centers without staff in attendance, and roads and buildings that do not exist, even though they were paid for, continue to belie the data showing positive growth for the continent as a whole.

New Public Management and other traditional reform tools designed for application in advanced countries were not able to answer this challenge. Large groups of citizens in emerging economies and low-income countries are still deprived of reliable public services in the areas that matter most, including access to clean water, hygiene and sanitation, health, and education. The sheer magnitude of the task of building, in a very short time, the kind of public services that took developed countries decades to create, and the lack of ideas about how best to use those facilities, have combined to sustain an intolerable situation.

Then the Arab world was rocked by revolution. Led by the young and technologically savvy, people across the Middle East and North Africa rose up to demand their human rights, essential services, and democratic governance. Instantaneous access to information through the Internet helped to mobilize the masses, uniting them in their demands and facilitating their activism. Although the revolution caught the world by surprise, the use of social media as a communication and rallying tool did not. People all over the world today use social media and mobile phone technology to share news, express themselves, and fight back. Facing corrupt and sometimes brutal governments, the Internet's social media outlets might be the only trusted communication link citizens have with one another and with their government.

Yet even in those countries, reforms were under way. Government information was becoming more widely shared through mobile technology. Government websites included information about where funds were spent, what was achieved with those funds, and where problems continued to baffle attempts at solution. Even in such countries as Afghanistan, Bangladesh, and Pakistan, governments were deploying communication technologies as a tool to improve government.

We authors have spent much of our professional lives assisting developing governments to implement public management reforms that in the end did not deliver, or at least did not deliver enough. Tony Verheijen's efforts to transplant successful developed countries' reforms to developing country contexts failed (partially) in many of the countries where he worked. However, even where that was the case, the appetite among reformers to learn and try to apply lessons from other contexts made the efforts important in their own right. The attempts of elected governors in provinces of the Democratic Republic of Congo to rebuild public services and delivery systems in the face of adversity and formidable challenges pushed him and his teams to do better and to seek solutions that are out of the box to address the highly complex problems they had to confront. He was inspired by the can-do attitude he had witnessed in many of the transition states in Central and Eastern Europe and their progress in rebuilding economies and societies. The question arose time and again, Why not in Africa or South Asia? Often the answer was, Your tools are not right for our conditions. Instead of dismissing that argument, we should be inspired by it to do better, especially in the face of the deep problems that remain in the Afghanistans, Burundis, and Democratic Republic of Congo of this world, or even in somewhat less dire but still difficult environments like Uganda, Tanzania, Bangladesh, or even Pakistan.

Jody Kusek's two decades of work in helping countries design, build, and use results monitoring and evaluation (M&E) data for better decision making were stymied in many countries by lack of trustworthy data, little commitment from leaders, and a culture of "hide the ball" rather than deal openly with what was working and what was not. Results-based M&E have not proved to be the panacea hoped for by the development world. Moreover, countries want to know how to implement programs and projects and how to do so without the possibility of failure. Years of designing Results Frameworks and Chains have not been the answer.

However, things are changing. When Zubair Bhatti was supervising the 20,000-plus government employees of Pakistan's rural district of Jhang in 2008, he spent considerable time reacting to unceasing throngs of petitioners. Despite being the person in charge, he had little control over the indifference of many of his subordinates to the citizens' complaints. Tired of not being able to do more to help the 3 million underserved citizens, he began on his own to pick up the phone and call the citizens who had visited his office complex for various licenses, registrations, and permissions. Because most people had cell phones, why not contact them instead of waiting for complainants to arrive in his office? The citizens of Jhang were more than surprised, shocked, and delighted to realize that the resident of the multiacre, 150-year-old, awe-inspiring colonial mansion in the heart of their city was reaching out to ask their opinion about the treatment they received during recent transactions.

It was just one isolated effort, one of innumerable such innovations attempted by interested officials across South Asia's vast public sector landscape. How to scale and institutionalize such innovations? How to get the political leaders and the civil service interested and sustain their interest? How to replicate such innovations in different service delivery contexts? How to demonstrate results? These were, and continue to be, the big public sector management questions. Six years later, with enthusiastic support from several champions, especially the Chief Minister's Secretariat and the Punjab Information Technology Board, that initial effort has gathered momentum. Several new ideas have been added, such as data collection with smartphones to monitor government employees in such jobs as inspection, facility monitoring, and extension. We have named this innovation the Smart Proactive Government model and describe it later in the book.

Because communication technologies were beginning to be harnessed for improved government in Punjab, Pakistan, we wanted to know: Did similar examples exist elsewhere in South Asia? How could a region so infamous for its problems with service delivery be at the forefront of innovative service delivery solutions? We also wondered: Were more traditional public management reforms contributing anything to the success of this effort?

Our purpose in writing this book was to share the remarkable technological innovations in public management systems taking hold in Punjab, Pakistan, and other places across South Asia, and more important, to identify key factors that made the innovations successful. Although we share a number of information and communication technology (ICT) innovations from around the world, we focus our analysis on the South Asian region because each of us has worked there, and we are thrilled to share good news from South Asia. The research for this book involved a review of nearly 200 ICT innovations. We were trying to identify a potential set of criteria (we call them "solutions") that were transferable from one region or country to another. Chapter 3 introduces five solutions that we found to be consistently present in the successful innovations we studied.

We use the word "solutions" with great humility. Having struggled for years with public sector complications, we understand that there are few recipes for reform and that context is king. If reform were an injectable medicine, we would have cured public sector ills a long time ago. After all, finding good laws and institutional structures is only one Google search away. Fortunately, most theorists, having struggled with failing to transplant modern institutions to developing countries, now acknowledge, just as most practitioners always argued, that replicating structures does not work. It is not about the form of institution. It is all about implementation. And implementation is hard—extremely hard. It is unglamorous and grueling and fraught with reversals, resistance, and reaction.

We could have written another book diagnosing the problems and suggesting high-minded solutions, such as "Sell when prices are high, and buy when prices are low," which is difficult to prove wrong but almost impossible to implement. We also understand the frustrations of the politicians and senior civil servants who are quite tired of the thousands and thousands of pages written by development organizations that describe problems in painstaking detail but fail to suggest concrete, feasible, cost-effective ideas to move forward. Five hundred pages of analysis of the stock market, with the concluding suggestion to "sell high and buy low" is not really a way forward.

We chose to focus on highlighting successful innovations that are helping to improve public management systems and the delivery of essential services for the benefit of the people. We include a section on the risks and challenges of introducing technological system reforms. Do not claim categorically that most of the innovations we describe caused long-term change in government, because very few of the reforms have been academically or scientifically researched. We do know that the recipients of these innovations claim that change would not have occurred without them.

Documenting successes from Afghanistan, Bangladesh, and Pakistan is another risky venture. Isn't Pakistan synonymous with conflict and militancy? How can it be incubating successful innovations? Can tinkering with cell phones here and there really tackle militancy? As we were completing the first draft in March 2014, the enormity of these obvious questions was driven home to us in the starkest possible manner when a dear friend, one of the few mainstream TV anchors arguing for a tolerant, liberal

Pakistan, barely escaped a shower of bullets from six assassins on a busy Lahore thoroughfare. His driver died on the spot. Militancy is certainly a challenge in South Asia, and the full range of state resources, from the army to foreign policy, from reforms of school curricula to the justice sector, taxation, and sanitation services, will have to be deployed to fight the menace, build state credibility, and restore citizen trust. Given that delivering improved services will be at the heart of any such effort, we hope that the solutions we put forth in this book, however humble or simple they may sound, may help to push progress forward.

We have many people to thank for their support through this process. They have helped us explore these questions. Many of our colleagues generously gave their time to review early drafts of the manuscript. We also feel honored to be able to share the many stories of innovations in public management, particularly those occurring in South Asia. We thank Omar Masud, Helene Grandvoinnet, Emiko Masaki, and Billy Hamilton for their generosity in providing us with thoughtful and timely peer review comments. Each of these very busy individuals was supportive and helpful to our effort. Not enough thanks can be given to Michael Trucano, a most sought-after expert on ICT systems in developing countries. Mike was our sounding board, our critic, and our friend throughout this venture. He contributed directly to the development of chapter 3. We also thank Charlie Undeland and Hafiz Naiumur Rehman for researching the India and Bangladesh case studies; Zainudeen, in Sri Lanka; Roland Clarke in Brazil; and Erwin Ariadharma and Maria Tambunan in Indonesia. We wholeheartedly thank Michael Soots of the GIS Department in Tillamook County, Oregon, for his time in developing the story on Tillamook. He also provided rich detail in remembering our visit there almost two decades ago.

Zubair especially thanks his young World Bank Islamabad colleagues for giving life to wild ideas, creating several innovations, introducing these ideas to other provinces, thinking through constant design improvements, and researching several parts of this book. Thanks are extended in particular to Asim Fayaz, Marium Afzal, Umar Nadeem, and Ali Inam, for co-creating this ambitious innovation agenda; to Ayesha Shahid, for researching and writing several case studies; and to Saad Idrees, Samar Deen, Saad Omar, Fahd Sheikh, Ameer Haider, Zahra Mansoor, Ayyaz Ahmad, and Shahryar Ahmad for the implementation in Punjab, Sindh, and

Khyber Pakhtunkhwa provinces. Many thanks are also due to Younas Dagha for sharing his Sindh water courses story, the first major ICT-based monitoring effort in the country, and to Dr. Shujaat Ali, for nudging him to document that efforts. Special thanks to Younas Suddique for providing excellent administrative support.

We also thank U.S. Ambassador David Robinson for his reflections on the role smartphones played in improving transparency and accountability during the 2010 parliamentary elections and more recent Afghanistan elections. Many thanks to the United Kingdom DFID Sub-National Governance Program for helping fund the World Bank technical advice.

Thanks from us all to Ellen Goldstein, Rachid Benmessaoud, Alphonses Marcelis, Onno Ruhl, Naseer Rana, Amit Dar, and David Wilson for providing a safe space to conceptualize an write this book.

We thank Pamela Johnson for reading the manuscript and contributing such a thoughtful foreword. Jody especially thanks Pamela for the many hours spent together over the last two decades discussing the importance of information in government service delivery. Her continued leadership in this area has been an inspiration to many government innovators who preceded her into government service.

Special thanks are due to colleagues at the Punjab Information Technology Board: Dr. Umar Saif, the dynamic young chairman, for jump-starting and steering the extremely ambitious ICT innovation agenda in the province; and Amir Chaudhary, Sajid Latif, Burhan Rasool, Fasieh Mehta, and Saflain Haider for tireless implementation and navigation of the complexities of change management.

Most important, many thanks are due to innovation-minded civil servants in government—Dr. Tauqeer Shah, Nabeel Awan, Mohyuddin Wani, Rashid Langrial, Farasat Iqbal, Azmat Mahmood, Imran Sikandar Baloch, Nasir Javed, Najam Shah, Waseem Ajmal, Mushtaq Ahmad, Imdad Bosal, Noor Mengal, Waqas Mahmood, Nadeem Mahboob, Saima Saeed, Hamed Shaikh, Saif Anjum, Zulfikar Hameed, Ahsan Younas, and many others—who work every day to try to expand the boundaries for the welfare of the average citizen in circumstances much more challenging than we in international development organizations imagine. Nothing would be possible without their passion, integrity, and dedication to public service.

About the Authors

Zubair Khurshid Bhatti has served as practitioner, manager, and thought leader in the public, nonprofit and private sectors for over twenty years. While serving in successively senior roles in Pakistan's Administrative Service he supervised the delivery of public services to remote Balochistan tribes, urban Karachi slums, and rural Punjab districts. As District Coordination Officer of the Jhang District, he supervised more than twenty thousand employees responsible for delivering government services to over three million citizens. He previously worked with the Baltimore Sun to help cover the 1989 student demonstrations in Beijing, the Asian Development Bank to advise on justice sector reforms, Engro Chemicals to manage corporate communications and social responsibility, and The Asia Foundation to promote social accountability. Currently, as Senior Public Sector Management Specialist with the World Bank he is using his vast experience to help design, implement, scale, sustain, and spread government and private sector innovations in cell-phone based citizen engagement and performance management.

Jody Zall Kusek has successfully worked with governments, NGOs, international organizations, and the private sector for nearly thirty years to help them make more evidence-based strategic and financial decisions. She has spent nearly twenty of those years advising developing and emerging economies on designing and implementing public management programs that deliver more effective and efficient results that matter to their citizens. Her work at the World Bank includes the co-development of a "Country Assistant" framework to assist the institution dialogue with clients on development priorities. Previously, she served as a director for two cabinet agencies in the United States Clinton-Gore administration in a similar capacity. She has published three books in the area of effective government management, along with numerous peer review papers, blogs, and book chapters. Her book *Ten Steps to Results Monitoring and Evaluation* is published in nine languages and is used by governments and universities across the world. In addition to her work at the World Bank, she continues as adjunct professor at the University of Maryland, School of Public Policy.

Tony Verheijen has worked for the last 25 years on public management and institutional reforms in Europe and Central Asia, Africa, and South Asia, as a development practitioner and scholar. He contributed to the process of European integration of Central and East European states in the 1990s and 2000s by providing advice and support to the management of their EU accession process and to the internal transformation of their institutional systems. He also supported governments in East and Central Africa on decentralization and service delivery reforms, focusing, in particular, on postconflict and transition countries. He has also held managerial positions, including as a regional program manager at UNDP, manager of the World Bank's Governance and Public Sector Management team in South Asia, and, currently, as manager of the Serbia World Bank Country Office. Apart from his work as a development practitioner, Tony Verheijen has held various academic and teaching positions in the Netherlands, Ireland, Belgium, and Poland. He has published widely on public management, constitutionalism, decentralization, and European integration.

Chapter 1

A New Citizen-Government Alliance

The most valuable commodity I know of is information.

—Gordon Gekko, Wall Street (1987)

The County of Tillamook, Oregon, located on the northwest coast of the United States, is known for its beautiful, rocky coastline, salmon fishing, and, of course, its famous Tillamook cheddar cheese. In 1998, while working for President William Clinton, one of the authors of this book was asked to go to Tillamook to find out what was behind several reports that this community worked well, solved problems, and had high citizen approval ratings.

Across the country, in Washington, DC, the president of the United States was promising to improve the people's trust in government. It seemed that Tillamook's leaders had already figured out one way to do this.

In addition, we heard that a Geographic Information System (GIS)—an information technology used by the U.S. military—was helping Tillamook to manage its programs and solve its problems. We were intrigued and wanted to learn more. Still, we wondered why we were flying across the country to a tiny community of cows, cheese factories, and salmon fishing when so many enormous problems were pressing elsewhere. Back in 1998, we didn't realize that effective governments were increasingly using data and information to help solve problems and restore citizen confidence. Tillamook proved to be a textbook example of how to do that.

County Commissioner Sue Cameron met us at the Tillamook courthouse and immediately told us how flooding of the pristine wetlands was ruining salmon runs and bird populations and endangering cows and people. During 1996, a torrential flood had caused $53 million in uncompensated losses; 700 dairy cows were killed, many families were displaced, and numerous homes and business destroyed. It was a disastrous human and economic blow to a county of 25,000 people, where the average annual income was only $18,000. Commissioner Cameron told us that what the community needed to solve the problem of flooding was reliable data. It needed to understand which were the most vulnerable locations in the county and what mitigation measures it could implement to prevent another disaster. Useful data were in short supply or nonexistent. Without reliable data, however, the county could not plan or manage its flood protection strategies or monitor whether or not they were working.

Despite its costs and a lack of trained staff, the county turned to a technology called a GIS to gather the needed data and determine what actions were needed to reduce the probability of another disaster.

A GIS enables various layers of data—which are often assessed separately—to be digitally mapped in a way that allows several variables to be seen simultaneously. For example, the location of key infrastructure or businesses could be mapped with historical rainfall levels and populations centers. To deploy the system Tillamook county officials would have to make a significant investment in new staff skills and in the purchase of the GIS mapping software and computers. Because GIS data could be transformed into easy-to-understand charts and graphs, county officials were able to mobilize public opinion and obtain the community's support for the necessary expenditure of tax dollars.

The next flood arrived on Thanksgiving Day 1999. Almost 10 inches of rain fell in 48 hours—a relentless repeat of the 1996 deluge. This time however, the community was prepared, thanks to GIS data. County commissioner Gina Forman said that damages were reduced by 96 percent and the county was overjoyed that not a single cow died. (govinfo.Library.unt.edu/NPR/Library/speeches/21st hammer/html).

In fact, in 1996, the year of the Great Tillamook Flood, a revolution in public management was already under way. Governments in the United States, Australia, New Zealand, the United Kingdom, and other developed countries were at the forefront of the changes, asking, What value are we getting for all the money spent on government services and programs?

It took another decade, but developing countries—often pushed by developed countries—began asking the same question. Citizens began pointedly saying, "Show me—don't tell me" where the money went. To be able to answer these questions, for themselves and for citizens, governments needed reliable data to enable them to monitor and

County commissioner Gina Forman said that damages were reduced by 96 percent and the county was overjoyed that not a single cow died.

What value are we getting for all the money spent on government services and programs?

evaluate how well policies and programs were working. As much as reliable data, decision makers need the data quickly—not months or even years after a program has been implemented or even, as in some cases, after the program ended.

Today, terms such as "evidence," "informed decision making," and "managing for results" have become part of the management lexicon of development practitioners. New funds now are rarely invested in programs without an accompanying framework detailing the expected results and what is to be achieved with the money spent. These tools and terms are the trademark of current development programs, but they cannot reliably claim the success or failure of a development program without information systems to produce reliable data.

Citizens Are Demanding More Accountability from Their Governments

Citizens throughout the world are demanding to know how well government is delivering services such as health care, education, waste collection, maintenance and building of infrastructure, and others. Citizens want to know how government spends their money, and they want the information to come directly from the service provider. Mobile and communication technology (ICT) has been a "game changer" by letting ordinary people log onto an Internet access device, such as a smartphone or tablet, and immediately communicate with government as never before imagined. Citizens in Karnataka, India, can go to the state government's website to find out how much money was budgeted for any key state program. In Kenya, citizens can learn that their national government has been funding a cross-cutting program to help prevent substance abuse. Information about which agencies contributed to the program and how much they contributed in the last or current budget year is also available online. Bangladesh uses its Citizen Voice (Nagorikkontho) program to empower the public to provide feedback about public services through a government web portal. After a citizen report was made about high entrance fees for the Panchagh Woman's College, the government investigated and found that students were being charged more than twice the approved amount. The Ministry of Education instructed the college to revise its fees.

Citizens in nearly all developed countries are finding out how well their governments are performing, how transparent they are, and whether the information they are providing is fact or fiction.

A government's reassuring, "You don't have to worry; we'll take care of everything for you," no longer works today. As one community planner put it, "If you want to stir up citizens, simply put forth the effort to shroud your government in secrecy." Access to the Internet through smart devices, such as a phone or a tablet, is on the rise in developing countries. The lack of tolerance for government secrecy likely will become even more prevalent in these countries as the price of smartphones continues to drop—possibly to as little as $20 per phone. Access to information is only a beginning! Information can help reveal the credibility of leaders in keeping their election promises. Using the Internet, people can gauge whether seemingly terrible services and inept public management systems are really as poor as they seem and whether leaders are corrupt and ineffectual, or not.

The new transparency that the Internet provides has led citizens living in some developing and emerging economies to take to the streets to vent their frustration with what they see as nonresponsive and corrupt political leaders and ineffective public sector management. Many such protests are rooted in poor delivery of public services.

The outpouring of citizen dissatisfaction is visible around the world. In some cases, demonstrations revolve around issues of security, such as the dismal performance of the police force in protecting women from harassment and rape in India. In Pakistan, rioting was sparked by lack of electric power in blistering summer heat. In other cases, the issue is urban development and safety. In Turkey, mass protests around Taksim Square in Istanbul were spurred by an urban renewal process that was seen as nontransparent and driven by greed (box 1.2). Similar protests swept across central Skopje (Macedonia). More critically, corruption-driven gross neglect of worker safety in Bangladesh, resulting in thousands of deaths, generated months of protests by large sections of Bangladeshi society (box 1.4).

Yet other protests have resulted from the prioritization of public expenditures for government-preferred, prestige programs like sports facilities over providing for basic social needs. Such was the case in June 2013 when mass demonstrations erupted in Brazil during the Confederation Cup. Citizens are tired of government impunity and shameless acts of corruption and are mobilizing to demand change (box 1.1). The hunger strike movement of Indian social activist Anna Hazare is another example of citizen activism. The strikes mobilized hundreds of thousands of citizens to push for citizens' rights and greater government transparency and to demand, among other things, that official corruption be investigated and punished (box 1.3).

Box 1.1

Bus Fare Hikes Trigger Massive Protests in Brazil

A hike in bus fares in Brazil triggered mass protests and vandalism in 11 cities across the country in June 2013. Deeper, complex causes of citizen disenchantment, however, lie in myriad issues of political corruption, growing inflation, and citizen dissatisfaction over the allocation of public funds for the 2014 World Cup and 2016 Olympic Games, set against continued restrictions on resources for social services. Despite Brazilian president Dima Rouseff's tough stance on corruption, bribery and fraud remain rampant. Brazil's middle class has been hardest hit by the rising prices of basic goods such as food and rent. In spite of Rouseff's reforms to address stagflation, reduced services, and reduced costs of hiring new government employees, a general sense of unease and declining prosperity grips Brazil.

Box 1.2

Using Social Media for Peaceful Protests in Turkey

The June 2013 "peaceful" protests in Istanbul, Turkey, were spearheaded not by the masses but by highly educated youths, who used social media to gain the respect and support of thousands of Turkish citizens, from high school students to middle-aged supporters. These protesters, the "youth at Gezi Park," are globally integrated and represent the westernized segment of Turkey. They were protesting against the prime minister's interventions into their private lives, including, for example, how many children they could have and what they could or could not drink. The group effectively explored the potential of information and communication technologies to enhance democratization. Even though they might represent the westernized minority, their message transcended Turkey's international borders and garnered global support.

Source: http://www.brookings.edu/blogs/up-front/posts/2013/06/13-turkey
-protests-gezi-park-democracy-kirisci.

Their message transcended Turkey's international borders and garnered global support.

Despite the many examples of citizen protest, poor governance systems in many countries have responded by riding out the storm. Although this may work in the short term, it won't stop the evolving changes in citizen attitudes that are manifest in growing social activism and greater willingness to actively protest. As Schmidt and Cohen (2013) note in *The New Digital Age: Transforming Nations, Businesses, and Our Lives,* public trust may initially decline, but it will emerge stronger as the next generation of leaders takes these developments into consideration.

Global Shifts—Catalysts for Change

The balance of power between citizens and their governments has shifted rapidly over the last decade.

Certainly it seems that the balance of power between citizens and their governments has shifted rapidly over the last decade. Governments no longer hold all the power or all the information. A number of factors are responsible. The authors identify five global shifts that have rearranged both the way citizens feel about their governments and the way governments approach interactions with citizens. These five shifts discussed below appear in the transformation of Tillamook, Oregon, where 25,000 citizens expected their local government to prevent flood damage, as well as in the massive demands for better government that have swept the countries such as India and Bangladesh.

Shift 1. Funding Results That Make a Difference
Walk up to any government leader and ask what keeps him or her up at night, and you are likely to hear, "Too little money and too many problems." You might also hear, "Too much money going to the wrong problems." Yet when the authors contacted a number of officials we have worked with in the past, we heard something else. We were told that far too often money was spent on diagnosing problems and coming up with bold, general recommendations. What they believed was needed instead was a set of feasible and specific, concrete solutions that could be tested and implemented immediately. In fact, we heard one official say that he needed concrete solutions that would "help me gather more votes instead of fueling more agitation." These problems are not new. For hundreds of years, developed governments have grappled with internal and external demands for improvements in the ways public funds are managed. Now, it is the developing countries that are facing pressures from a global economy that is trying to squeeze out waste and demanding

Box 1.3

Protesting a Brutal Rape

The India's Daughters Campaign represents Indian civil society's effort to use mobile technology to mobilize youth, specifically those from girls' schools in the most rural areas. The campaign protested the brutal rape and murder of a 23-year-old medical student in the capital city of the world's largest democratic country. Multiple social work organizations, along with the Study Hall Educational Foundation, took to the streets in February 2013 to protest and to educate young people about gender bias and the state's responsibility to make the streets in India safer for women.

Source: http://www.studyhallfoundation.org/campaign/.

Box 1.4

Unsafe Factories in Bangladesh

Rana Plaza was an eight-story commercial building near Dhaka, the capital city of Bangladesh, that included a shopping center and five garment factories. In April 2013, Rana Plaza collapsed, killing an estimated 1,100 people. Approximately 2,400 others escaped or were rescued from the rubble. It was clear that the collapsed building had had structural flaws that violated structural codes and that labor laws were also being violated. Reportedly the majority of commercial buildings in Bangladesh do not follow any building codes. Factory owners and government officials who failed to properly regulate, monitor, and enforce building codes were criticized in Bangladesh and internationally. Locally, protests and citizen pressure on the government culminated in the closure of 19 unsafe factories.

Source: http://www.economist.com/news/asia/21577124-tragedy-shows-need -radical-improvement-building-standards-rags-ruins; http://www.economist.com /blogs/schumpeter/2013/05/factory-safety.

to see results with diminishing resources. The pressure is seemingly from everywhere: parliaments, citizen groups, the private sector, nongovernmental organizations, and, of course, from the richer countries that continue to invest in them.

The clamor for greater accountability and more effective government is part of the conversation among development professionals around the globe. It started among Western countries, and now demands are rising in developing countries where states often have failed to deliver even fundamental public goods such as property rights, roads, basic health, and education. We believe that most governments want to invest taxpayer monies to deliver programs that citizens care about. But many governments, and citizens alike, would agree that for far too long the right questions were not being asked, questions such as, What does success look like? and How would you know it was being achieved? (Kusek and Rist 2004). Results-based management (RBM) was hailed as the cure-all for demonstrating to citizens and other stakeholders that governments were indeed using the public purse for activities to improve people's lives. Today, the largest push to move the RBM agenda forward in developing countries comes from international partners such as the World Bank, the United Kingdom's Department for International Development (DFID), and other multilateral and bilateral donors. With every development program competing with others for the same resources, these donors are insisting that spending on any program produce results that citizens both want and need.

Thus donors have spent hundreds of millions of dollars helping developing countries establish structures and systems to measure everything from the numbers of children staying in school to the number of rural mothers delivering their babies with a qualified health provider.

South Africa, for example, is investing significant resources in designing and implementing its results-based planning and program model. The effort began during President Jacob Zuma's first administration and emphasized improving delivery of services across South Africa. Twelve national goal areas were agreed upon, covering everything from improving infrastructure and the national skills supply to health care. The country was able to identify key performance goals and which departments were principally responsible for achieving them. South Africa is admirable in having established an accompanying evaluation program to determine if the effort was having any effect on service delivery and government performance. It determined that funding would go to what is working and that what is not working will be fixed.

There are plenty of other examples, such as activities in Brazil, Colombia, Malaysia, and now India. Over time, results-based management has shifted the development dialogue to greater focus on demand and less on donor supply. And one of the building blocks of results-based management is trustworthy data. To produce the data, governments are investing in monitoring and evaluation (M&E) systems to supply the evidence of what works and what does not. In most countries, to design, build, and use M&E systems is a significant challenge. Many of the systems being built, such as the one in India, are elaborate and encompass the entire government. Regardless of the design chosen, a monitoring and evaluation system must be able to collect, analyze, and transmit data quickly, to enable a decision maker to assess whether programs are on track or off track and whether new problems are apparent. Being able to monitor and evaluate programs is one of the most important jobs of any government, but it only works if the data being used are timely, reliable, and, most important, sufficiently detailed to make it possible to devise the right solution.

Funding would go to what is working and that what is not working will be fixed.

Monitoring and evaluation only works if the data being used are timely, reliable, and most important, sufficiently detailed.

Shift 2. Electronic Communication Technology Available to Everyone

The explosion of mobile phones across the world is a well-known story today. We authors are old enough to remember the excitement of buying our first mobile phone, easily eight inches from end to end, with the ability to reach very few people and costing more than $500. In 1999, approximately 25 million people worldwide were using a mobile phone. Having a phone then was mostly aligned with being wealthy or part of the government elite. Today, there are more than 650 million mobile phone users in Africa, and close to 3 billion across Asia. "If the current pace of technological innovation is maintained, most of the projected eight billion people on Earth will be online," argue Schmidt and Cohen (2013).

Mobile technology is significantly expanding the capacity of government to deliver services to citizens and businesses. The most notable progress has occurred in developing countries, which historically have been limited by poor or nonexistent communications infrastructure, impeding economic development and social improvements. Mobile technologies are enhancing the value of government services, from an electronic credit card to pay taxes, utility bills, and the like, linked to a mobile phone in Bahrain, the United Arab Emirates, or the Philippines; to voting, registration, or electronic monitoring in Morocco, Kenya, Estonia, and Ukraine. Mobile technologies support farmers with weather and market price alerts in Malaysia, Uganda, India, and China, and they feed location data to emergency responders in Turkey, the United States, and France (OECD/ITU 2011).

In a number of developing and emerging economies, such as Kenya and Bangladesh, mobile technology is being used to distribute information to citizens. Emergency messages, such as "A cyclone is coming; seek shelter," are saving lives. So are messages reminding pregnant women not to forget to come to their prenatal appointments. Much of the information is static, so that interaction with citizens is limited. But this type of mobile government does provide real-time communication with citizens and can also create cost savings for both governments and citizens. In another example of this type of communication, Bangladesh provides emergency flood warnings via its short message service (SMS), and China provides similar warnings of typhoon dangers.

Governments also have used mobile technology to expand two-way interactions between citizens and governments. Citizens can complete transactions with government at their own convenience electronically. Examples include self-service options for paying taxes or making other types of payments, booking appointments, and even applying for grants or entrance into universities. In Turkey, citizens can query and pay their taxes via SMS and can also register to receive a reminder of their tax payment deadlines and the amounts due. Brazil's SMS registration for government job seekers gives notice of a job match and 24-hour notice to candidates to show up for an interview.

According to Daniel Lathrop (Lathrop and Ruma 2010), in his book *Open Government: Collaboration, Transparency, and Participation in Practice,* digitally enabled e-government strategies delivered some important benefits. It made government information and services more accessible to citizens while creating administrative and operational efficiencies. But too many of those initiatives simply paved the cow paths; that is, they focused on

In Kenya and Bangladesh mobile technology is being used to distribute emergency information to citizens.

automating existing processes and moving existing government services online.

With free access to information about budgets, infrastructure, health, sanitation, and education, it is possible to make decisions based on real data never before available. "It's a game changer," argue Schmidt and Cohen (2013).

Mobile Service Delivery as a Gateway for Integrated Governance

In 2012, the Indian National e-Governance Plan announced a framework for mobile governance. The strategy and its implementation are intended to make use of available wireless and new media technology platforms, mobile phone devices, and applications for delivery of public information and services to citizens and businesses. The Department of Electronics and Information Technology initiated work on a mobile service delivery platform, dubbed "Mobile Seva," to enable any central or state government department to deliver both web- and mobile-based services seamlessly to citizens. As of mid-April 2014, Mobile Seva had made possible the delivery of 299 public services via citizens' mobile devices. Mobile Seva has been used approximately 2.2 million times.

The SMS Gateway is a short message service or SMS. One service that has recently been popular is the voter information check, to verify whether a voter's name is on the electoral roll of a constituency and locate the designated polling station. In addition, departments have used "push services" to send notifications or alerts to citizens. Thus far, 980 central and state government departments have used push services to send 777 million messages to citizens. More than half of the messages relate to two subjects: farming and the new identity system.

A Mobile AppStore, launched in January 2012, now hosts 295 live mobile applications or apps. The most popular app downloads are Right to Information Directly, India Post Status tracking, Election Commission of India (ECI) polling station location, ECI tracking of electronic voting machines, and national identity enrollment status. Another popular application, Rakshak, was built specifically for the safety of women and senior citizens. In an emergency, the click of a button sends an SMS message with the person's location to four different numbers of relatives or friends and a voice call to the emergency response number of the local police.

India's Mobile Seva made possible the delivery of 299 public services via citizens' mobile devices.

The fully government-owned Unstructured Supplementary Service Data (USSD) channel has been commissioned to provide "notify and response" services. Unlike SMS messages, USSD communication makes possible live exchange of information. It does not require an Internet connection and works on low-end-technology phones, making it ideally suited to deliver services to the poor. Proof of concept pilots have been initiated by the governments of Maharashtra and Kerala for the delivery of designated services. The USSD channel has been formally recommended for financial services use, such as tax or other bill payments. The feasibility of its use for wage payment to the tens of millions of poor workers in the national rural employment guarantee scheme is being explored.

Many government department services involve some form of payment. A mobile payment gateway, PayGovIndia, has been developed for making electronic payments. PayGovIndia has been made available to government departments and agencies for integration with their applications.

E-Purjee: Delivering Sugar Buying e-Vouchers to Farmers in Bangladesh

With more than 200,000 sugarcane farmers spread around Bangladesh, managing information flow was one of the biggest problems confronting both sugar mill owners and farmers. Sugarcane harvesting and crushing are time-sensitive operations that sugar mills and farmers need to manage efficiently to ensure that no sugarcane crop is lost because of delays. The *purjee,* the paper voucher sent to farmers by sugar mills advising them to bring their cane for crushing, sometimes took days to reach farmers, causing them to miss the crucial time window when they needed to reach the right sugar mill so as not to lose too much sugar content in their crop. The *purjee* system has been in place for over 200 years, despite its problems. "The traditional system was not very transparent, with some farmers not receiving their *purjee,* jockeying by some farmers to manipulate the system, and rent-seeking middlemen. Delays in delivery reduce the weight of the cane and hence income of the growers. The unpredictability of the system also impacted the efficiency of the mills" (Minges, Raihan, and Raina 2011, 11).

Bangladesh Food and Sugar Industries Corporation automated the *purjee* for quick and efficient notifications to farmers when sugar mills were ready to receive their output. Farmers receive an

SMS message telling them to bring their cane to the mill and another
one informing them when they are to receive payment. The SMS
messages are more than a communication tool. They also act as
authorizations of the amount of raw sugarcane a farmer is expected
to supply (usually 1,200 kg) to a particular mill at a defined date
(Alam and Wagner 2013a; 2013b). To ensure the smooth functioning
of the system, growers are asked to preregister their (or a relative's)
mobile numbers with the sugar mill.

Piloted in 2009, the initiative was expanded to all 15 sugar mills
in Bangladesh by 2010. Several studies have found significant impact
on sugar production from this simple solution to the problem of
information asymmetry. Alam and Wagner found that sugar mills
are now able to crush fresh sugarcane typically within 24 hours of
harvesting, resulting in a 7.5 percent increase in sugar recovery, and
that "the digital procurement system increases growers' economic
gain over the paper based system."

Perhaps more important, Alam and Wagner found that the success
of the *e-purjee* system was due to its acceptance by the farmers.
The added reliability of the digital system created the impression of
transparency and fairness, especially for the small farmers, whose
ability to cope with system failures is not as great as big farmers'.
This "procedural and distributional fairness, as well as uncertainty
reduction in *purjee* distribution," turned out to be most important to
the small farmers, who often were not aware of the monetary gains
the new system brought. The study also found that another reason
for high acceptance of the system was that it relied on a mobile
phone-based SMS, a technology that was already widely accepted
(Alam and Wagner 2013a; 2013b; see also box 1.5).

Shift 3. Open Government Seals the Transfer of Power to Citizens
Cow path or not, "open data could be the game changer for developing
countries to improve decision making at all levels of government,"
blogged Craig Hammer (*Harvard Business Review*; blogs.hbr.org,
March 29, 2013). Lathrop and his colleagues wrote that "open
government in its most basic sense is the notion that the people have
the right to access the documents and proceedings of government"
(Lathrop and Ruma 2010, 1). An explosion of new media technologies,
increasingly vocal and vigilant advocacy groups, enhanced donor
attention to good governance, and sustained pressure for openness are
necessary to create the shift from secrecy to transparency.

Open government is widely seen to be the mark of contemporary democratic practice and is often linked to passing of freedom of information laws.

Box 1.5

The Sri Lanka "e-Revenue License" (eRL) Success Story

There are currently nearly 4.8 million vehicles in Sri Lanka, nearly 25 percent of them registered in the Western Province. The Department of Motor Traffic (DMT) issues nearly 1.2 million motor vehicle revenue licenses annually (essentially a vehicle tax) or about 5,000 per day. The tax yields annual government revenues of 2.2 billion rupees or $17 million.

Obtaining a revenue license used to be onerous. Vehicle owners had to go to the particular divisional secretariat where the vehicle had been registered and spend half a day to finish the process. Revenue collection centers would manually validate supporting documents, such as insurance policies and emission test certificates. In addition to the hassle for citizens, the system had several shortcomings for the government, including the lack of a mechanism to detect forged documents, the inability to track vehicle transfers between jurisdictions, and inefficient revenue collection.

The government reengineered the business process to develop a centralized, web-based system that allowed citizens to file online for a revenue license. The service allows citizens to select their insurance company and emission company. It then checks the citizen's vehicle against the respective insurance and emission company databases, and upon confirmation of validity, allows users to apply electronically for renewal. Citizens pay for the license using a credit card and can print a receipt. The Western Province Department of Motor Traffic sends an original revenue license to the citizen's home by post.

This e-revenue license (eRL) service was developed by Sri Lanka's information and communication technology (ICT) agency, which also developed a one-stop e-shop for other government services (http://www.srilanka.lk). Since its inception in 2009, nearly 1.5 million vehicle owners have been served by the system. Approximately 2,411 online users have obtained their licenses, and 98 percent of the users have found the service to be highly satisfactory. Reengineering older work processes, along with the ICT–enabled new processes, reduced the time required from hours in a divisional secretariat to two minutes by computer.

The service is expected to expand to other provinces. A mobile payment system has also been established that sends a text message notifying people of the expiry date of their revenue license and the need to renew. These measures are expected to rapidly increase the number of online users in 2014.

Source: World Bank.

Open government is widely seen to be the mark of contemporary democratic practice and is often linked to the passing of freedom of information laws. Scandinavian countries claim to have adopted the first freedom of information (FOI) legislation over 200 years ago (Anders Chydenius Foundation 2006).

The difference between a government with a freedom of information law and a government with an open data or open government law is that FOI requires a process to be established in a country that is "document-centric." It requires a person to request a document that has already been produced and another person who "audits" the process to determine the document's degree of secrecy or privacy and whether or not it can be provided to the requester. The process is intended to create less secrecy and more transparency. A country that has opened its data has agreed to create a process that is not based on someone's requesting a specific document, but which provides access to all government information products in its system, present and future, and possibly even those from the past.

India's 2005 Right to Information Act is considered one of the most empowering and progressive laws of this kind. Its implementation has been upheld in landmark judgments by the Central Information Commission related to the records management of public universities, property statements of civil servants, and grades earned by people taking the civil service preliminary examinations (CUTS International 2010).

India's Right to Information Act is considered one of the most empowering and progressive laws of this kind.

Shift 4. Social Media Gives Voice to the Elites as Well as to the Poor
Amir Haten Ali's seminal paper "The Power of Social Media in Developing Countries" (2011) describes in perfect detail the role that social media has had in shifting the balance of authority from government to ordinary citizens. On January 28, 2011, Egypt's president, Hosni Mubarak, took the drastic step of shutting off the Internet for five days across the entire nation. His purpose was obvious: to halt the flow of communication over social media platforms such as Facebook and Twitter and thus the coordinated assemblies that were taking place. That Mubarak took such a desperate step demonstrates the power of social media and its ability to get data and information into the hands of citizens about government as has never been done before. Prior to the first day of protest, 85,000 Egyptians pledged on Facebook to attend "Revolution Day." In the two weeks leading up to and including the first few days of the protest, Egyptians created 32,000 Facebook groups and 14,000 Facebook pages (Fowler 2011).

The effect of social media on the Arab Spring is still being studied, but we now know for certain that as a result of its connecting people and groups from around the globe, the formal institution of government as we once thought of it is no more. And as Jude Hanan (2013) of the World Bank blogged, "Social media makes information porous. National borders, government structures, or even languages are no longer relevant in this new environment." As Schmidt and Cohen (2013) put it, "while this is hardly the first technological revolution in our history, it is the first that will make possible for almost everybody to own, develop and disseminate real-time content without having to rely on intermediaries."

Shift 5. A New Generation of Leaders Who Use Technology Will Make a Real Difference in People's Lives
Imagine the tremendous possibilities if connected leaders could address their governments' future problems. This shift has not happened yet, but the authors believe it will be the most important to occur in the 21st century. Look at only one example: "In 2012, the MIT Media Lab tested new mobile technology in Ethiopia by distributing preloaded tablets to primary-age kids without instructions or accompanying teachers. The results were extraordinary: within months the kids were reciting the entire alphabet and writing complete sentences in a foreign language [English]" (Schmidt and Cohen 2013). These connected kids will be the next cohort of government leaders. They will likely be helping to solve the problems of delivering public services with the aid of technology.

A number of countries around the world are embracing—and bracing for—a new group of leaders who will think about problems and how to solve them in ways that their parents might not have dreamt of. In the United States, for example, President Barack Obama laid out a comprehensive government reform strategy in 2014 with technology at its center. His strategy sets out to accomplish three things: (a) to enable the American people and an increasingly mobile workforce to access high-quality digital government information and services anytime on any device; (b) to ensure that as the government adjusts to a new digital world, the opportunity will be seized to procure and manage devices, applications, and data in smart, secure, and affordable ways; and (c) to unlock the power of government data to spur innovation and improve the quality of services.

After creating the massive telecom infrastructure—from cheap handhelds to inventive bill payment mechanisms to maintenance of towers in remote locations—the private sector is also helping to drive this shift. Through its technology information board (the PITB), Punjab is working to establish fast and cheap e-payment mechanisms to open new avenues for entrepreneurs and is

Using technology to solve government problems is one of the most important shifts of the 21st century.

soliciting input from citizens on how to improve service delivery and identify corruption. It is also working with industries and universities to foster online innovation in Punjab.

How Have These Shifts Affected South Asia?

Although these five shifts have occurred around the world, we are particularly interested in the changes that have transpired in a number of countries in the South Asia region, which is home to one-fifth of the world's people and the highest percentage of the world's poor. Although the World Bank classification includes Afghanistan, Bangladesh, Bhutan, India, the Maldives, Myanmar, Nepal, and Pakistan as making up the region this book will focus on reforms and innovations from India, Pakistan, Bangladesh, and Afghanistan. This "subregion" has enjoyed two decades of growth and has an increasingly vocal middle class that has loudly asked for performance from the parties in power. The results of the last two elections in India and Pakistan are cases in point, in which the voters elected parties appearing to perform well at the state level to the national government with strong majorities.

Despite those developments, however, these states still have public sectors with institutions that often seem to be frozen and immovable, combining political-level grand corruption with administrative and petty corruption. But they also have high rates of adoption of information technology. Although Internet penetration in the region still hovers below 20 percent, mobile phone penetration has reached record levels. Some 90 percent of the populations of India, Pakistan, and Bangladesh have mobile phone coverage. Each of the three largest South Asian countries has more than 60 mobile phone subscriptions per 100 people. Tariff rates are among the cheapest in the world. Since 2009 Pakistan has consistently ranked among the top countries in small message service (SMS) usage. In fiscal year 2012–13, a staggering 315.7 billion SMS messages were exchanged by mobile users there. India boasts more than 65 million Facebook users, the second-largest national community after the United States. Pakistan has some 8 million users of Facebook (the Statistical Portal, statistia.com /statistics/193056/facebook).

The latest development has been the introduction of cheap smartphones based on the Android platform. According to Mediacell, a London-based consultancy group, India has about

States still have public sectors that seem frozen and immovable.

156 million smartphone users among its population of 1.2 billion. The number is expected to more than double to 364 million in 2014. Equally significant, 92 percent of the 224 million forecast sales of smartphones in 2014 are expected to be sales to new users. In short, a computer with power matching NASA's when it launched the first man into space is available in Colombo, Delhi, Dhaka, Lahore, and Kabul for less than $50. Some 84 million of India's 100 million users access Facebook from their mobile devices. With such affordability, use of smartphones is rising rapidly, as is general familiarity with them. The $40 Aakash tablet, made by the British-Canadian company DataWindwill, also is helping to spread smartphone use. Aakash is an Android-based tablet computer promoted by the government of India as part of an initiative to link 25,000 colleges and 400 universities in an e-learning program. The Indian government has purchased 100,000 of them, and they already exceed Apple's market share in India. The combination of India's planned drastic improvement in Internet connectivity from cities to villages and the availability of cheap smartphones and tablets is expected to increase India's Internet penetration rapidly in the coming decade.

The following story, told by Jennifer Bussell in her recent book on India, makes a strong case for advancing information and communication technology (ICT) in South Asia:

> I watched a young woman enter a small store in a shopping mall in Raipur—the capital of one of India's poorest states, Chhattisgarh—to collect a birth certificate. She had submitted a request for the certificate a few days earlier, using the store's online application system. When she returned, the woman paid a small fee, and the storeowner printed the official document. In total, she spent only a few minutes applying for and receiving her birth certificate, which she would need to access myriad basic government services. At that same location she could have obtained many other essential documents and services as well, from a caste certificate or driving license to a land ownership record or welfare benefit. Only a few years earlier in Chhattisgarh, this same woman would likely have faced a much different environment when attempting to access a similar public service. She almost certainly would have needed to visit multiple government offices to collect the

relevant documentation, and when she was finally able to apply for the certificate, she might have been asked for an additional "fee" to speed up the process. Even if she paid this bribe, it would have taken perhaps a month for her to receive the official document. (Bussell 2011, 1)

Linking Citizens to Government

Pakistan reached 70 percent mobile phone penetration in 2013, with most phones costing under $60. In Sri Lanka, there are over 19 million mobile phones for approximately 20 million people. Because more than one-third of Sri Lankans make their livelihood from farming, the government introduced a program to provide timely SMS messages to farmers about current market prices and new seeds and fertilizers. Other messages sent to farmers are related to the availability of vocational education, health education, and nutrition.

In Punjab, Pakistan, the government has shown true leadership in its willingness to "own" a public management system in which many program decisions that affect citizens are made using data collected directly from citizens. Called "proactive governance," the "citizen feedback model," or the "Jhang model," this innovation involves government's seeking feedback directly from citizens on services delivery, introducing mandatory smartphone use by service providers, and creating dashboards with current information showing services delivered, where they are delivered, and how citizens perceive their quality.

The proactive governance system was introduced in 2011 and works on the premise that government should ask citizens about the quality of services delivered to them. By noting citizen mobile phone numbers when services are provided, and following up through robocalls and SMS messages, service providers create a direct line to clients. The fundamental logic of this system, which makes it different from traditional grievance redress and complaint handling systems, which also exist in Punjab, reduces the scope for gaming by both sides. More important is the change of relationship between service provider and citizen, which was previously unimaginable: The citizen is not coming to the state; the state is coming to the citizen.

The citizen is not coming to the state; the state is coming to the citizen.

It is important that mandatory smartphone use by service providers removes the onus from citizens, who would otherwise have to complain if they did not receive the service they were entitled to, creating the risk of gaming and blackmail on both sides. Instead the

Information is changing the balance of power between citizens and government.

responsibility is on the service providers, who must both prove that they went to the location of service provision and take before-and-after pictures as proof that the service was delivered. This system was started in a small number of sectors and is now being rolled out more widely. The rapid fall in the price of smartphones makes it affordable.

Another reason why the authors found studying South Asia particularly interesting is that in our nearly 70 collective years studying governments, and our more than 45 years working specifically in developing countries, we have yet to find a group of countries so deprived of the trustworthy data needed to support good public sector management. For that reason, using results-based management (RBM), in the current sense of the phrase, is not realistic in many of these countries. Yet we are finding excellent examples of trustworthy and real-time data being channeled to decision makers for evidenced-based decision making. They are not only recent innovations; some have been operating for some time (see box 1.6).

It is also encouraging to find a number of South Asia countries, primarily Bangladesh, India, Pakistan, and Sri Lanka, starting to break down the wall of secrecy that separates state institutions from citizens. These countries are taking advantage of the many changes occurring in other countries with respect to the rights to information and more openness in government. That citizens have both the tools and the right to demand and obtain information is changing the balance of power in the relationship between citizen and government. The change applies to different countries in different degrees. It is significant in India and less so but evolving in Bangladesh, Nepal, and Pakistan. Yet the very fact that the right to information is acknowledged makes a fundamental difference.

We have also seen many public sector reformers in India, Pakistan, and elsewhere in South Asia using mobile communication technologies to address seemingly intractable public sector monitoring and citizen engagement problems. Box 1.7 describes how mobile technology was used to reduce new cases of dengue fever in Pakistan by over 80 times.

Nowhere are the gains more visible than in the rapidly growing use of digitized information and social media in Pakistan. The public sector has lagged the private sector, but it is now recognizing the advantages of new technology. Working with local banks, national

Box 1.6

Monitoring the Monitors: Verifying Work on Sindh Water Courses in 2006

The use of communication technologies to improve monitoring of government projects is not new, but it is becoming more commonplace. Since 2007 the Punjab Irrigation Department has successfully employed structured text messages sent by third-party monitors to resolve complaints of water pilferage by upper riparians. The text messages, which a monitor sends directly to a central server, include reports on water flow and water thefts, among other indicators.

Text messages relay digital data in real time but cannot provide irrefutable evidence. As early as 2006, the Sindh chapter of the National Program for Improvement of Watercourses (NPIW) implemented near-real-time, location-tagged, photo-enforced monitoring. Established in 2004, NPIW aimed to reduce water distribution losses by straightening and partly cementing watercourses, the last "retail" outlets of the area's massive irrigation network. But managing an operation of more than 6,000 rural locations spread over 150,000 sq km was a challenge. Obtaining good field data was key.

In 2007, the Sindh unit digitally mapped the irrigation network to enable foolproof identification of the watercourses being improved. Ten teams of field monitors with iPAQ devices—previously known as "pocket personal computers"—sought real-time data on the watercourses directly from the field. They developed a single-screen supervision tool, eliminating multiple layers of paper data aggregation and transfer. Multiple tiers throughout the government had access to the same data through a single screen and at the most basic level. The process eliminated delays, inaccuracies, and mistakes in data aggregation.

Was it easy to implement? Not at all, says Younas Dagha, the enterprising director of the Sindh effort (pers. comm.). Expensive devices were procured from Dubai; specialized software was written; the national space agency was contracted for satellite images; and extensive training was held. Maintenance and replacement of the iPAQ devices were tricky. Yet those obstacles were overcome and the project was delivered successfully.

This high-tech monitoring initially required specialized devices and software. But the rapid penetration of smartphones has since made the same operation much easier, as well as more accessible for many organizations with less capacity. Dagha, now the chief secretary of the sparsely populated and mountainous Gilgit-Baltistan region, is introducing the same successful ideas, with much greater ease, into the education, health, power, and food departments in that region.

In Punjab, the irrigation department, which has used the SMS-based digital data for some time, will be including smartphones in its service. The same timely data will be produced, but with the advantage of unchallengeable date, time, and location information and photos documenting water levels and episodes of theft. Are the monitors charging too much for petrol? The distance-traveled gauge on their motorbikes is also required to be photographed before and after daily field trips. Are repair and maintenance activities difficult to monitor? Use smartphones.

Source: World Bank.

Box 1.7
Fighting the Dengue Mosquito in Lahore

Unlike nearby New Delhi, the dengue mosquito had not bothered Lahore—until 2011, that is. In early 2011 Lahore faced a dengue epidemic. Practically every household in the city was affected. The news media were full of frenzied accounts of ever more citizens suffering and dying. With dengue mosquitoes breeding in freshwater in gardens, flowerpots, and air conditioners, the rich and the upper middle classes, usually immune from the health challenges of the masses, were not spared. That the fever didn't discriminate contributed to the sense of crisis heard in every street corner conversation.

Facing a political disaster in his core constituency, the chief minister of Punjab, Shahbaz Sharif, sprang into action. No resources were spared. Everyone was enlisted into the anti-dengue fight. City authorities and the health department focused on training doctors, providing platelets, conducting blood tests, and providing indoor care. Education officials instructed children in schools, and the information technology department organized help lines. The fisheries department imported dengue-eating freshwater fish from Egypt, and the information department launched a massive information blitz. The intelligence wing of the police reported on the various government activities.

In the field, the government focused on a range of fogging, larviciding, and de-ponding activities, but the demanding chief minister was dissatisfied. He wanted to know the progress of the implementation and to root out problems and fix them. One immediate problem was that GIS spatial data indicating where new infections were occurring were not being collected. The idea of using smartphones to monitor anti-dengue activities and where new cases were appearing was suggested and was implemented on a small scale. But the dengue season was ending. With the immediate crisis past, the urgency to do new things also petered out.

But dengue returned the following season. The government asked Dr. Umar Saif, the youthful, newly appointed chairman of Punjab Information Technology Board (PITB), to come up with a solution. In addition to immeasurable energy, Saif brought academic experience and a penchant for thorough analysis to the anti-dengue fight. When the dengue season started, PITB developed a powerful smartphone app. It provided dengue-tracking teams from all departments with smartphones to record their dengue fighting activities with geo-tagged pictures that could be displayed live on a map on an online dashboard. Once data started coming in, Saif oversaw analysis of the data with a special algorithm that combined occurrences of dengue larvae with data on where dengue cases were emerging most rapidly, to pinpoint areas in which to focus preventive activities.

During 2012, as in the 2011 dengue season, almost every department in Lahore was single-mindedly focused on anti-dengue activities, except this time, they were all being recorded on smartphones. Little pins representing each activity conducted started emerging on the dengue dashboard, which the chief minister could track in daily meetings to ensure that no vulnerable or affected areas were neglected. The ability to predict which areas were vulnerable further strengthened the government's ability to focus its activities and prevent major outbreaks.

(Continued)

> **Box 1.7** *(Continued)*
>
> In 2012, a total of 258 confirmed dengue cases were diagnosed in Lahore—a drastic reduction from the previous year's 21,000 cases, a number widely considered to be an underreport. By 2013, Lahore's anti-dengue activities had evolved further. The government of Punjab had identified some of the most prolific dengue breeding areas to be graveyards and junkyards in monsoon seasons. It assigned different departments to focus on certain sites only. By the end of summer 2013, the dengue patient tally in Lahore remained similar to that of 2012, even though the virus had visibly spread to the neighboring district of Sheikhupura, in Rawalpindi, and even in relatively distant Swat and Karachi. Rawalpindi and Sheikhupura have already started smart-monitoring of anti-dengue activities. In Punjab at least, one thing is clear: as the dengue virus spreads out of Lahore, so do the smartphones and smart-monitoring tools needed to meet the menace.
>
> Source: World Bank.

police are using mobile money to pay some officers and allow them remote access to their accounts via mobile phone. The program is still in its infancy, but in a country that routinely lands near the bottom of Transparency International's annual corruption survey, reliable, accurate financial transactions mark an important step forward.

The police also are extending their eyes and ears through a new Emergency Services Call Center. With rapidly growing mobile phone use, private citizens—many in remote areas with little permanent law enforcement presence—can give the center information about caches of weapons, explosives, or other dangerous items. The police have been responsive to the calls, and use of the center increased by more than 17 percent in the last calendar year. At the same time, police are experimenting with a literacy phone project for policewomen. Early results show that women who used the literacy phone app showed marked improvement in literacy rates. Not surprisingly, those who did not use the app showed little or no improvement.

Box 1.8 describes how technology was put to use in the 2014 elections in India.

Remarkably, we are also finding reason for optimism even in the most fragile South Asia countries, such as Afghanistan. Unlikely as it may seem, and despite working against tremendous odds, Afghanistan also may have entered its transformational decade. Advances in health, education, women's rights, and technology

Box 1.8

SMS-Based Poll Monitoring in the 2014 General Election in India

India has just completed the general election 2014—the mammoth and astoundingly complex democratic process involving 814 million voters. Elections in the world's largest democracy pose immense challenges with respect to logistics and man and material management. Information and communication technology (ICT)–mediated tools, especially mobile phone-based applications, were extensively deployed to provide electors easier access to information, for greater transparency, and for better election management.[a]

The challenge is to gather information in real time from widely dispersed polling stations, many in remote locations. To tackle this issue the election commission implemented SMS-based monitoring to track the entire election process at the polling stations—from the dispatch of polling parties until they return and deposit the EVMs and other election materials. The SMS-based poll monitoring system used coded messages to track data at all 930,000 polling stations in the country.

Explaining the efficiency of this process, the deputy election commissioner, Alok Shukla, said, "Officials on the ground just need to punch in a few letters to send various coded SMSes. The information is instantly available online and can be used by the commission and poll officials in the state capital and districts."[b]

Notes

a. The Election Commission of India Announcement of General Election 2014 (March 2014).

b. http://www.thehindu.com/todays-paper/tp-in-school/smsbased-system-to-help-poll-panel-monitor-2014-elections/article4281038.ece.

will be hard to reverse, even as the country continues to struggle with an aggressive insurgency. A recent poll showed that more than 68 percent of Afghans believe that the country is firmly on the right path and that the vast majority reject a return to the Taliban era.

As it did in India, technology played an active part in preparations for Afghanistan's April 2014 presidential and provincial elections. Earlier votes had been tainted by widespread fraud, including ballot box stuffing and tampering with vote tally sheets. In the 2014 election cycle, campaign agents were equipped with smartphones and took photos of completed tally sheets displayed at polling sites, establishing a baseline to detect fraud at the final count. Journalists armed with smartphones also filed reports directly to their publications' websites, providing real-time accounts of how the elections were proceeding. Having this smartphone data was the

Box 1.9
Afghanistan Elections

In the September 2010 parliamentary elections in Afghanistan a large number of candidates competed, and margins of victory were close. Unfortunately, that created opportunities to shift electoral outcomes by tampering with vote counts. Electoral institutions were weak, and accountability of election officials was limited. If they chose, they could help corrupt candidates increase their share of votes. There was also a history of candidates' taking advantage of patronage networks to manipulate voter counts.

During the elections (Wolesi Jirga elections), Callen and Long (2013) set up a randomized experiment to try to prevent fraud in the counting of votes. To measure fraud, they made sure that at each voting station the provisional vote tally sheet was photographed, and then they compared it to the vote totals reported for the station. They found that fraud at the vote counting stage was rampant. There were discrepancies in 78 percent of the data they recorded, and parliamentary candidates associated with the election officials in charge of the vote counting received a disproportionate share of the fraudulent votes.

The study also implemented an experiment to discourage election fraud. In a randomly selected subset of polling stations, the researchers sent a letter in advance announcing that they would be photographing the provisional vote tally sheet and comparing it to reported totals. The intervention reduced aggregation fraud considerably. Furthermore, the loss of votes by politically connected candidates was disproportional: they lost about 25 percent. Candidates connected to the officials in charge of aggregation in their constituency also lost votes disproportionally in this experiment.

Source: Callen and Long 2013.

reason election fraud was identified early after the run off votes were cast (personal conversation).

Although still struggling to achieve its development goals, after decades of nearly continuous warfare Afghanistan shows distinct signs of sustainable progress. Technology that makes government more effective and accountable and that helps citizens exercise their rights with confidence is a worthwhile tool (see box 1.9).

Some governments are implementing technology-based fraud reduction methods on a large scale. And some are first experimenting and piloting different methods. But the direction of change—especially given the impetus from a new cohort of young, assertive media users, pressure applied by the middle classes, and the ferment of the new anticorruption political parties—is unmistakable. The rapid spread of communication technologies, such as the feature phone, the smartphone, GIS, and the like, will irreversibly change the public sector, as technology is doing in many other sectors of everyday life.

The rapid spread of communication technologies, such as the feature phone, the smartphone, GIS, and the like, will irreversibly change the public sector.

References

Alam, M., and C. Wagner. 2013a. "Assessing the Impact of Digital Procurement via Mobile Phone on the Agribusiness of Rural Bangladesh: A Decision-Analytic Approach." *Agribusiness and Information Management* 5 (1).

———. 2013b. "Motivating Acceptance of Information and Communication Technologies in Rural Agribusiness: It's Not the Money." Proceedings of the Sixth Annual SIG GlobDev Pre-ICIS Workshop, Milan, Italy. http://www.globdev.org.

Ali, A. H. 2011 "The Power of Social Media in Developing Countries." *Harvard Human Rights Journal* 24: 1.

Anders Chydenius Foundation. 2006. "The World's First Freedom of Information Act Celebrated 2 December 2006." Anders Chydenius Foundation. http://www.Chydenius.net.

Bussell, J. 2011. *Corruption and Reform in India, Public Services in the Digital Age.* Austin, TX: Cambridge University Press, 1.

Callen, Michael, and James D. Long. 2013. *Institutional Corruption and Election Fraud: Evidence from a Field Experiment in Afghanistan.* Unpublished working paper 9. Center for Effective Global Action, University of California Berkeley. http://Cega.berkeley.edu.

CUTS International. 2010. *Analysing the Right to Information.* Briefing paper. http://www.consumersinternational.org.

Fowler, Geoffrey A. 2011. "Facebook Sees Egypt Usage Spike." *Wall Street Journal*, February 2. http://online.wsj.com/article/SB10001432405274870477560457612047424761857.8.html.

Hanan, Jude. 2013. "Using Social Media for Good Governance" (blog), December 26. blogs.worldbank.org/publicsphere.

Kusek, J., and R. Rist. 2004. *Ten Steps to a Results-Based Monitoring and Evaluation System.* Washington, DC: World Bank.

Lathrop, Daniel, and Laurel Ruma, eds. 2010. *Open Government: Collaboration, Transparency, and Participation in Practice.* Sebastopol, CA: O'Reilly Media, 1.

Minges, M., A. Raihan, and R. Raina. 2011. *Access to Information (A2I) Evaluation, October 2, 2011.* UN Development Programme, Bangladesh. http://erc.undp.org/evaluationadmin/reports.

National Performance Review. U.S. government. "Coastal Oregon County Learns Value of Partnership with Feds." govinfo.Library.unt.edu/NPR /Library/speeches/21st hammer/html.

OECD/ITU (Organisation for Economic Co-operation and Development and International Telecommunication Union). 2011. "M-Government: Mobile Technologies for Responsive Governments and Connected Societies." OECD Publishing. http://dx.doi.org10.1787/9789264118706-en.

Schmidt, Eric, and Jared Cohen. 2013. *The New Digital Age: Transforming Nations, Businesses, and Our Lives.* New York: Vintage, 2.

Chapter 2

Learning What Makes Government Work in the 21st Century

The illiterate of the 21st century will not be those who cannot read and write but those who cannot learn, unlearn, and relearn.

—Alvin Toffler

Pick up the most recent *The Economist,* or even the *The Wall Street Journal*, or check out a blog from the abundance devoted to international development, and you will likely see yet another story about a failed public management system. It is no surprise to most of us working in international development that in many developing countries there are still plenty of schools without teachers and health clinics without doctors. We can remember images of roads paid for but not built, and in one egregious example, the runway next to President Sese Seko Mobutu's village in the Congo that was long enough to accommodate the Concorde. Why, we ask, have not decades of public sector management reforms and billions of dollars spent created efficient, well-functioning governments? Why the protests? Why so little trust in government?

Yet in many of these publications one is just as likely to find a story about a new mobile phone app intended to solve the problems of failed government systems. Confusing? Certainly! Where is the disconnect?

Why, Despite Reforms, Is Trust in Government So Low?

At the 2012 United Nations General Assembly meeting it was reported that despite the miserable economic performance of the West over the previous few years, the global fight against poverty had made progress. The proportion of people living on less than $1.25 a day has dropped from nearly one-half, to around one-fifth, in the last 20 years. Worldwide, the number of children who die before reaching the age of five was halved over the same period (*Bloomberg BusinessWeek Global Economics*, September 22, 2013).

Why hasn't this good news translated into more trust in government?

One reason is that in many countries there is a groundswell of citizen outrage over the performance of government and leaders who seemingly look the other way. The growing demand for better performance is taking many forms. As discussed earlier, India experienced a wave of activism in 2012, when sloppy policing, nonresponse by emergency forces, and substandard treatment by a health center led to the death of a victim of violent rape. In a blunt message to other world leaders, Narendra Modi, running on a platform of reform, was elected India's prime minister in May 2014, and his BJP (Bharatiya Janata Party) won a sweeping victory in Parliament taking over the majority of seats.

In Brazil, anger at corruption and inappropriate priorities in government expenditure policies, particularly investment in sports stadiums instead of schools and health services, and general dissatisfaction with the inability of government to deliver basic services spilled into the streets of São Paulo and other major cities during the 2013 Confederation Football championship.

In Turkey, anger over opaque government decision making and poor performance expressed itself in violent opposition to the destruction of a beloved public park to make way for a shopping mall. A remarkably similar story played out in Skopje, in the former Yugoslav Republic of Macedonia, about a month later.

In Bangladesh in 2013, mass demonstrations rattled the government when lack of enforcement of workers' rights led to the death of more than 1,000 workers in a fire in a garment factory.

All of these are examples of governments failing to provide basic services, such as security, protection of the vulnerable, property rights, public transport, and water and sanitation. Beyond the cases that made it into the international media are many other examples in which increasingly empowered citizens have challenged government priorities and performance. Citizens have been helped in their protests by the availability of social media, which facilitates much more rapid and large-scale mobilization than would have been possible in the past. Thanks to technology and increasingly widespread open government legislation, citizens know much more about their rights to public services and are thus more able to hold the public sector accountable. To this much more vocal and informed

Why hasn't good news translated into more trust in government?

citizenry, government response has in many instances been at best a form of containment, and not the introspection and effort necessary to respond substantively to legitimate public grievances. For example, the Turkish protests were followed about six months later by major purges in the Turkish police, ostensibly as a response to allegations of corruption.

For many developing and emerging economies, and in particular for South Asia, the answer to the question of why government is so underperforming for its citizen often defaults to lack of political will; competing priorities, such as security; lack of funds; and too many vested interests. Those are standard excuses for retaining service delivery systems that deliver rents to politicians and officials who restrict service access to those willing to pay a premium to officials but deliver few services to those who need them most.

Considering the persistent and rising demand for governments to deliver, and looking at ominous historical patterns of inadequate response to citizen dissatisfaction, one may say that the odds are that eventually, politicians who ignore the mismatch between demands and supply do so at their own peril. In many countries there are indeed legitimate concerns about security, economic management, and other issues, but getting services out to citizens has to be a priority on the same level as those other concerns, and in the end, a contented citizenry is in political leaders' self-interest.

How can decision makers heed the demands of citizens and be responsive, while avoiding revolutions?

The classic remedy is either punishment or reward at the ballot box. However, it is well known that other factors come into play in elections. Despite recent examples of success by novice political forces with anticorruption and service delivery agendas, such as the Pakistan Tehreek-e-Insaf (PTI) political party in Pakistan and the Aam aadmi (AAP) Party in India, it remains unwise to rely on elections alone to focus attention on improving service delivery (box 2.1).

After Decades of Public Sector Reforms, Few Victories Can Be Claimed

Voting for or against a candidate is certainly a remedy for reform, as is citizen uprising. Still, we think there ought to be mechanisms to improve service delivery within existing governance systems, that is,

Box 2.1

Responding to Demand: The Rise of New Political Movements

The political landscapes of emerging economies are often characterized by "frozen" configurations of traditional political forces that simply reinvent themselves from time to time. "Peronists" in Argentina are probably the best-known example, but the same goes for left-wing parties in Brazil, the African National Congress (ANC) in South Africa, India's Congress Party, and others. Among emerging economies, few such systems are as firmly fixed as those in South Asian countries.

In Bangladesh, Pakistan, and India, the same political dynamics have played out over generations. But something new has been happening in recent elections. Protest movements have developed into political parties that have become forces to reckon with. The PTI, led by former cricket champion Imran Khan, is the fastest growing political party in Pakistan. The PTI's ballot success in 2013 enabled it to form the government of Khyber Pakhtunkhwa, one of Pakistan's provinces. The AAP, or "common man's party," led by former tax inspector Arvind Kejriwal, captured the government of New Delhi in December 2013, campaigning on issues such as better water and electricity supply (although the party gave up power after only a short period in government). Both movements-turned-political-parties are driven by voters tired of corruption and frustrated by unanswered demands for better public services.

It is still early to tell whether such activist groups will become permanent political forces or will be captured by the same system they are vehemently opposing. But that outsider political forces, campaigning on a service delivery agenda, could play roles as significant as those have done was unimaginable only a few years ago.

Source: World Bank.

without revolutions. Why is it so difficult to design government services and systems in line with what ordinary citizens demand? One answer is that many public administration systems have long histories of being focused elsewhere. South Asian countries, for example, have retained public administration systems shaped in the traditions of former colonial powers, albeit molded in local traditions. The systems were created to ensure enforcement of the laws, to administer justice, and to create and maintain basic infrastructure. Thus they focus on respect for due process and hierarchy and reward years of service over merit. Nor have they traditionally placed the needs of the citizen over the need for tight bureaucratic control. It seems that traditional systems often were contributors to the many difficulties that have arisen in attempts to introduce change in the status quo.

Prime Minister Margaret Thatcher's attempts to take on the British civil service provide an example. Thatcher tried to use her legal prerogatives to decide (not just sign off on) senior civil service appointments, as a way to create a more managerially oriented civil service. That was initially considered a breach of customary constitutional principles. Longevity of service was a common road to promotion, and claiming a new appointment by being first in line was also common practice. Thatcher's proposed change caused uproar among civil servants, lawyers, and academics, though interestingly, not among the general public. As on many other issues, Thatcher managed to outlast the resistance and set new precedents of active political involvement in top-level administrative appointments, ensuring the appointment of administrators who were like-minded and supported her preoccupation with effective management.

Thatcher's successor, Prime Minister John Major, and other leaders of developed countries were smitten with introducing public management reforms. A popular book called *Reinventing Government,* written by Americans David Osborne and Ted Gaebler in 1992, offered ideas on reforms considered by Major and others that spoke not to what government should do but how government should work (see box 2.2).

Yet despite the new ways in which governments are interacting with the public and managing their operations, the civil services of Bangladesh, India, and Pakistan remain firmly closed systems, with entry at the junior level and socialization through the ranks. That is equally true of civil service systems in Indonesia and Turkey, for instance, though less so in Brazil and South Africa. Attempts at substantial reforms remain outliers, such as the United Kingdom's "Next Steps," New Zealand's 1990s radical antidote to a failing economy, or even Tony Blair's "deliverology" (Schick 2003; Verheijen and Coombes 1998). Deliverology is the notion that introducing a top-level unit that troubleshoots and holds departments accountable for results better focuses the minds of

---

Box 2.2

The "Reinventing Government" Agenda: Osborne and Gaebler

More than 20 years ago, Osborne and Gaebler published their revolutionary book *Reinventing Government* to offer solutions for a more "entrepreneurial" government. In such a government, budgets no longer encouraged wasteful spending, and the "customers of government" took priority, not the bureaucracy. The public purse funded real change, not just deliverables, and governments leveraged the market to fund key activities. The book mainly describes local government experiments with managing diverse services, from recreation facilities to waste collection and reducing environmental damage, and how partnerships and competition helped local governments especially to do more with less. The book was also a call for the public sector to rethink historical "certainties," such as permanent employment (especially of service delivery personnel), and to break taboos such as merit-based pay (though Osborne and Gaebler did not support performance pay for teachers). It became an instant best seller and influenced governments the world over with its ideas.

Source: Osborne and Gaebler 1992.

---

managers and service delivery staff. "Delivery units" are now an increasingly mainstream tool. They have been introduced in diverse countries and settings, but especially in emerging economies, though instead of the temporary structures originally intended to troubleshoot and focus minds, they are increasingly becoming permanent enforcement features (World Bank 2013). Most other countries retain public sector management systems that continued to plod along with little thought to experimenting with newer models being tried elsewhere.

Holding public officials accountable for promises made or even just doing their jobs is a thorny problem in many developing countries. It is reasonable to assume that when we send our kids to school, a teacher will be there ready to teach them. It is also not out of line to anticipate that when we seek help at a health facility, a medical professional—even a doctor—will be available and equipped

Holding public officials accountable for promises made or even just doing their jobs is a thorny problem in many developing countries.

to diagnose and treat our problem. Yet we know that teachers in public primary schools in Uganda are absent 20 percent of the time. When present, they manage to actually train less than 20 percent of the day (Chaudhury et al. 2006). "In addition to being emblematic of problems facing poor people in developing countries, the failure of governments to deliver adequate services can be explained by failures of 'accountability' at various points in the chain of relationships in the implementation of policies, programs, and services" (Walton, Devarajan, and Khemani 2011).

The 2004 *World Development Report* (WDR): *Making Services Work Better for Poor People* advanced the idea that problems in the delivery of basic services, such as teacher absenteeism and leakage of public funds, could be the result of breaks in the long route of accountability. This route is a typical one in public management, in which citizens hold policy makers accountable for allocating resources and setting priorities, and they in turn hold service providers accountable for delivering services. This long route of accountability is one that takes time, depends on several actors for success, and lets many who ought to be held accountable when things go wrong or when programs fail "off the hook." The authors of the World Bank report have argued that holding service providers accountable directly to beneficiaries can help improve the delivery of those services. They called this the Short Route of Accountability. Take the example of a person buying a sandwich directly from a street vendor. Here one can decide immediately if the service is good, if the sandwich is tasty, and if the price seems right. Depending on their expectations, they are free to decide on the spot if they will come back or go somewhere else the next time they are hungry.

In many countries, not only are public officials not held accountable for poor service, but also the civil servants who are employed to deliver those services have few incentives to show up and fulfill their responsibilities. If teachers are paid regardless of their performance, and few penalties are handed out for absenteeism, then many will not show up. For middle and senior government managers, a gap often exists between the jobs that are expected to be done and the payment awarded. The underpayment argument is a tenacious one that has proved hard to dismiss. The salaries of civil servants in India and Pakistan are the equivalent of a few hundred dollars a month, at best, and can be even lower in other developing countries. Security of tenure, at the same time, is high. There is little or no risk of dismissal, even for underperformers. Low wages and guaranteed tenure lead to underperformance.

At face value, the salaries of public servants in emerging and developing economies tend indeed to be low, at least in absolute terms. But increasing resources alone is not the magic bullet for improving infrastructure, increasing access to and quality of public services, and ensuring security. The case of Pakistan illustrates this point. Pakistan ranks among the countries with the lowest revenue-to-GDP ratios in the world, around 10 percent. That may come as a surprise to many, inasmuch as Pakistan has a large industrial base, a strong agriculture sector, and some thriving commercial centers. Yet little revenue goes to the state for a number of reasons. The income tax, which is a critical part of overall revenue, only covers a fraction of the population, and most within that fraction benefit from numerous exemptions. Pakistanis in high-income groups, who in principle can contribute more, are contributing very little to revenue. The tax administration system is outdated and fragmented, with customs, income tax, and other operations not collaborating with one another. Numerous efforts to strengthen cooperation have all failed, and it seems that government is not interested in improving revenue performance. The situation is so bad that it recently led the U.K. Parliament to question its own government as to why Pakistan is the United Kingdom's largest development assistance beneficiary, when the country's own citizens clearly don't wish to contribute to the same development objectives by paying taxes (www.publications. parliament.uk, June 17, 2013).

Pakistan is of course not alone in having an extremely low revenue-to-GDP ratio. Bangladesh's performance is almost as weak. India fares somewhat better, but it is still far from the revenue mobilization levels of its fellow BRICS countries Brazil, China, Russia, and South Africa. Brazil, Russia, South Africa, and also Turkey have ratios in the 20 percent range. In all these cases, the fact that most people are employed in the informal sector combines with a lack of willingness to pay taxes and a weak tax collection enforcement regime to make increasing resources an uphill task.

Recruitment and career management systems are another part of the traditional puzzle. Countries that gained independence in the middle of the last century inherited their civil service systems from former colonial regimes, along with the idea of public service impartiality. In South Asia, in particular, the notion was subsequently

But increasing resources alone is not the magic bullet for improving infrastructure, increasing access to and quality of public services, and ensuring security.

translated into career management systems that left little room for discretion in decisions on career management by administrative leaders or politicians.

That inheritance has had two important consequences that negatively affect service delivery performance: First, closing off the civil and public service from competition (except at entry) and predefining career paths with scorecards for performance caused systems to evolve with a preoccupation for process instead of results. That problem is not limited to developing and emerging economies, or even to specific regions, but it has created a pattern of behavior that has proved very hard to undo. Second, with mainly self-managed civil service systems, the only instrument left for politicians to consolidate their own power is keeping senior officials dependent on their whims by using their prerogative to manage personnel rotations. The use of rotations is particularly significant in South Asian countries, where senior members of the subnational and central civil services are often rotated as often as every six months, creating the kind of leadership vacuum that prevents a focus on delivery or results, even assuming that the civil service elite were interested in either.

Civil service systems apply merit-based tools for recruitment, but other elements of the career management system stand in the way of that translating into better performance in service delivery. Political leaders and senior civil servants are caught in a revolving door that at best distracts from performance and at worst fuels corruption.

Researchers have studied the problem of staff simply not showing up for their jobs and not delivering the services that citizens expect. Many empirical studies have pointed to a dysfunctional interface between middle-level managers and service delivery staff as a critical cause of weak service delivery (DeRenzi et al. 2012; Banerjee, Glennester, and Duflo 2008; World Bank 2012). But even service providers who are present can still provide poor services. Absenteeism is only one element of poor service delivery, but it has been seen as a good place to start making a change. Over the last 10 years, numerous experiments have focused at the field level and on service providers and their closest administrative line managers.

One such initiative, by India's Udaipur district and the nongovernmental organization (NGO) Seva Mandir, made an effort to combine incentives and punishment and internal accountability measures to improve attendance by nurses in medical centers. Described in box 2.3, the case illustrates not only the deep-seated

Box 2.3

Udaipur District Internal Accountability Reforms and Why They Did Not Succeed

In Udaipur district in Rajasthan, India, survey responses showed that 75 percent of the population were using private medical services rather than free, government-provided care. In a district that is rather poor, this was quite a stunning number, but unfortunately not unusual across India and Pakistan. Of course, if these citizens pay the little hard-earned money they have for what they should be getting free, they cannot spend it on other important things such as schoolbooks for children.

The main reason why citizens opted out of the free health service was that there were simply no nurses on duty in most medical centers, so it did not make sense even to try to obtain services there. The district authorities understood that to start attracting citizens to public medical centers, the presence of a nurse practitioner would first have to be ensured. It was agreed that a monitoring system would be put in place that would track the presence of the nurses each day. A similar effort had been employed to combat teacher absenteeism in an NGO-run school in the same state, with some success.

The monitoring mechanism included a password-protected stamping machine that would record attendance. It was agreed with middle-level district managers that they would enforce sanctions on delinquent nurses and administer rewards for those nurses who put in their required number of hours. A well-known NGO was brought in to conduct the monitoring and report the information to the managers. The information provided would be impartial, limiting the perceived risk of abuse or blackmail by managers at the district level.

The system worked, and attendance doubled within six months, from 30 percent to 60 percent. However, 12 months later levels had fallen back below the initial baseline level, and the number of citizens using the health centers reverted to previous levels.

- The nurses found a way to get around the system by breaking the stamping machines, initially not sending them in for repair, and claiming "exemption days," which are days when they were supposed to perform other duties.
- Meanwhile, direct line managers and district middle managers did nothing to prevent the abuse of the system and explicitly condoned a growing number of "exemption days."
- No interest in the experiment was evident higher up in the chain of command.

Unsurprisingly, the experiment was abandoned.

Source: Banerjee, Glennester, and Duflo 2008; World Bank 2012.

nature of the problem of absenteeism, but also the limitations of internal accountability–based reforms that only deal with one part of the chain of command.

Strikingly similar results emerged from a study in Tanzania, where visiting community health workers' routines were monitored through SMS messages in a similar setup using an NGO. In that case too, after an initial response, community health worker performance in the long run did not improve (DeRenzi et al. 2012).

What those two internal accountability–based reform efforts achieved was to (a) generate better data on the actual performance of field workers and explain why government services were not working, and (b) improve our understanding of the dynamic that underlies the performance issues. They did not resolve the performance problems they had been designed to address, however. There were still no nurses on duty in Udaipur's medical centers and no medical practitioner visits to poor families in rural Tanzania.

Both of those experiments lacked a link to senior managers, such as the secretaries or directors in central ministries at the top of the hierarchy. In top-down, procedure-oriented systems, that matters a lot.

The New Public Management: A Theorist's Dream and a Practitioner's Nightmare

In *The Global Public Management Revolution,* Don Kettl (2005) reviewed many of the public sector reform movements of the previous 20-plus years. One effort, which has won and lost many followers, was a set of reforms introduced in the early 1990s called the New Public Management (NPM). Those reforms stemmed from the basic economic argument that government suffered from the defects of monopoly, high transaction costs, and information problems that bred inefficiencies. Among other things, the movement believed that by substituting market competition and market-like incentives, government could be shrunk, costs could be reduced, and performance could be improved. It offered not a single best option but a menu of options that countries could use to reform their public administrative systems, such as performance contracting, human resources downsizing, improved information technology, increased privatization, creating quasi-autonomous agencies to give managers more flexibility in pursuing goals, instituting customer service standards, and increased privatization (Kettl 2005).

Unfortunately, despite a rousing reception, particularly in Europe, little or no formal evaluation was undertaken to see whether any of the recommended steps made any difference. In time, the effort as a cogent set of reforms lost its followers. Moreover, some applications, such as user fees and downsizing, were disasters and became closely aligned to the failed structural adjustment programs of the late 1990s (Larbi 1999).

Other ideas from the New Public Management continue to be discussed, although not in an organized way. Letting the private sector provide essential government services, and thus doing away with some or much of the public sector system, is still being tried in a number of places, despite the fact that private companies have often failed to deliver the promised essential services and consequently, in many cases, contracts have been canceled. The much-maligned privatization of railway systems in Africa—and their collapse when private operations did not keep their part of the deal—is another example. Yet another is the sanitation problems that were created by contracting out waste collection in some African cities. Few poor people benefited from that scheme, as the effort often focused on picking up trash in wealthier communities. If developing and emerging economies are to keep growing, neither abandoning an inadequate public sector management system nor staying with the status quo is a reasonable option. Rather, as argued by Schick (1998), the basics of the public sector management system need to be fixed.

Results-Based Management: Show Me the Evidence

New Public Management also advocated making improvements in information technology and fostering effective government-citizen relations. Such a program was first launched in the United Kingdom in the early 1990s as a series of standards for key public services. Other countries, including Australia, Canada, India, and Malaysia, developed their own programs. Behind what were called "charters" were promises that the government would voluntarily publish information on how well services were being delivered and whether they were meeting the performance standards set in the charter. Citizen charters were considered success stories in some countries, and they were the forebears of today's "smart" efforts to refocus bureaucratic machinery on delivery. Out of them came a focus on evidence-based or fact-based decision making and what is now referred to as "results-based management" (RBM). As developed countries made RBM a reform mainstay, they also began asking what results were being achieved with the aid they were investing in developing countries.

Developing countries were also seeking realistic ways to be responsive to funding partners and other stakeholders with respect to what results were being achieved with their money. Brazil and Korea pioneered RBM instruments in the early 2000s, and Indonesia and Thailand followed with their own approaches (boxes 2.4 and 2.5). In Africa, such countries as Kenya, South Africa, and Uganda have led the way, at least in their rhetoric, and have selectively applied some RBM tools, including contracting between central units and line ministries and contracting between ministries and facilities, as well as performance incentives. Malaysia attempted to leap ahead with "delivery labs" to unblock complex service delivery problems. Malaysia is now putting government resources and commitment behind a scheme to link its national budget with programs that deliver results. After having

---

Box 2.4

Bureaucracy Reform: Indonesia's Ambitious Blueprint Shows Progress against the Odds

Indonesia's Bureaucracy Reform Road Map appears to have a good chance of proving wrong some conventional wisdoms, such as the notions that ambitious strategies always fail, especially in civil service reform; that creating winners and losers does not work, especially in a society like Indonesia's; and that gaming and cost will undo the process. Putting together a plan anchored in some rather ambitious and externally measured high-level performance indicators, setting and largely sticking with criteria that ministries must fulfill to join the reform process, and forcing a rethinking of the bewildering number of performance targets for ministries set by the ministry of planning are all difficult things to do. Nevertheless, so far Indonesian reformers have delivered on them. Certainly there was friction, even among the reformers themselves, and even more so between reformers and external experts brought in to advise and review. The process of winning over skeptics among politicians, and especially among senior officials, was often difficult.

The search for the right way to get ministries to assess their progress was long and in the end settled on the Common Assessment Framework developed for European Union countries. However, there are few other examples of countries that started with a large and ambitious framework and progressed as far as Indonesia in their goals. The critical test of success or failure remains whether, in the end, citizens receive reliable services. In areas such as customs and tax administration, signs are clear that that is happening. If it also happens in such areas as education, health, and sanitation, Indonesia may find itself an unlikely good practice case for results-based management.

Box 2.5

Brazilian Success in Results-Based Management: What Explains It?

Brazil has emerged as an unlikely good practice case in public sector management, in particular in transforming service delivery. A country with a historical reputation for weak fiscal management and ineffective public expenditure policies, Brazil in the last decade has generated some powerful state-level stories that show that performance-based management can indeed do what management consultants and donors claim. The Brazilian state of Minas Gerais has become a household name for those studying performance management. The states of Ceará, Rio de Janeiro, and Pernambuco have followed in its steps. The four states have gone farthest in introducing RBM-based public management systems, though they started from very different institutional and economic endowments. All responded to popular dissatisfaction with public services and a sense of having run out of options.

In two sectors that have been the targets of results-based management efforts in all four states, education and security, there is some evidence of significant improvements in outcomes in the short and medium term. The same goes for other sectors in, for instance, Minas Gerais, which has rolled out results-based and public management systems across a spectrum of public services. But even at the current level, the use of performance data to drive budget and staffing decisions and overall management of the public sector might be considered revolutionary, considering the states' past records.

It should be emphasized that in all four cases the performance management reforms introduced were part of a broader package of fiscal reforms that included investment in strengthening planning and budgeting, as well as efforts to depoliticize the civil service.

Source: World Bank 2013, 10, 31.

long resisted the introduction of RBM tools, India has since 2009 implemented its own variant of RBM, and Pakistan, Bangladesh, and Sri Lanka have shown growing interest in the approach.

Academics and practitioners debate the impact of results-based management reforms on public administration systems. They argue about whether RBM is a needed catalyst for mentalities in entrenched systems or is instead a set of instruments that serve to aggravate abuse and corruption.

Supporters argue that talking about results and obliging institutions to set targets and discuss them publicly will establish a positive feedback loop that will eventually help address structural problems in the public sector. They believe RBM will force institutions to think in terms of results-based approaches and methods. The risk of gaming when institutions themselves define their result targets is in this case seen as a lesser evil than retaining the status quo.

Regardless of one's viewpoint, either concept of RBM's role is meaningless unless the country can collect trustworthy data. Unfortunately this is where RBM breaks down, and reporting and using data are even more problematic. Even in richer countries, these systems report data far too infrequently to permit rapid decisions about programs or even policies. In earlier studies the authors have reviewed scores of results-based systems and tools being used in developing countries, principally in Africa and Asia. We found that many, if not most, developing countries we studied did not have the ability to use large, elaborate data systems, even ones designed, built, and funded by others. The reasons were (a) lack of skill capacity, (b) lack of commitment, (c) lack of incentives to make informed decisions, (d) overdesigned, overelaborate systems that made little sense in the local environment, and (e) lack of trustworthy data (Gorgens and Kusek 2010). For every Brazil, Malaysia, or Indonesia, we have a Solomon Islands or a Bangladesh. For the latter two countries, it was impossible to report on how programs were working or how services were being delivered, primarily because of lack of trustworthy data and little investment in developing a citizen-focused culture of governance (World Bank 2012; 2013).

Information Links Citizens to Government and Government to Citizens

What happens when service problems arise and government managers need to know immediately what is happening on the ground? Take the case of Arif Ahmad Khan, head of planning and development in Pakistan's Sindh province. Khan was recently confronted with the need for immediate and trustworthy information to defend his water filtration program. He could barely hide his frustration as he met with his senior staff. Khan had just received a call from his boss, who was most urgently concerned with the performance of the water filtration systems in the eastern part of the province's Thar Desert. Important constituents were complaining, but Kahn could not provide accurate information as to the problem. It was not the first time this had happened, and although he managed a billion-rupee portfolio of programs, which were mostly implemented by field managers, Kahn had very little firsthand knowledge of how well the programs were working. Nor was he regularly alerted when problems occurred. "I have no idea what's going on in my own districts, with irregular reporting, untrustworthy data," he told his staff. "What do I do?"

This time, a number of community elders had complained to the chief minister that some 20 reverse-osmosis water filtration plants across the vast expanse of Tharparkar, a sparsely populated desert district, were not working. This contention was contrary to the claims of the department responsible for the plants' maintenance. The elders alleged that corrupt officials were charging for water without running the plants. The chief minister wanted to find out whether the water plants, much needed in a parched land lacking sweet subsoil water, were working or not.

Managing with Trustworthy Data

Given direct verbal orders by the chief minister, Khan tasked a senior official with an immediate inspection to check the status firsthand. Two days later, the official reported that the allegations were false. He had seen two plants and they were just fine. But that answer did not satisfy Khan. In the past his inspectors had provided incorrect reports because of lax attention to the job. What Khan needed was trustworthy data that reported on the actual performance of every water plant. How would he get that when he knew that local officials often rigged the inspections by selectively visiting a couple of working facilities, or visiting ones made functional for the inspection, or quite possibly bribing the Karachi official? "I expected my inspector tasked with this assignment to personally visit every site, and he comes back after seeing only two. What do I tell the chief minister?" (story is based on personal communication).

This lament by managers is familiar and oft-repeated. From district officers to department heads to chief ministers to presidents, all complain about "flying blind." To provide them some sight, huge sums have been invested in building elaborate monitoring and evaluation systems. Has the investment worked? Unfortunately the answer is no, or at least, far from fully. What is seen instead is frequent recurrence of a vicious cycle as follows: A problem is identified; an attempt is made at fixing it; the fix does not resolve the issue; the failure is met with complacency, followed by declining state credibility.

The development goal of using data to support management decision making is still far from a reality. Delivering visible improvements without good monitoring data is difficult. Feasible, replicable, scalable, cost-effective solutions are scarce. Getting things done in remote rural hamlets, or even in sprawling urban slums, day in and day out, through tens of thousands of somewhat recalcitrant staff, without good information to guide a creaking chain of command is extremely hard.

Monitoring and Evaluation Needs Rapid Feedback

Over the last decade the World Bank and other development organizations have spent significant funds helping countries design and build monitoring and evaluation systems (M&E) to assess the progress (or lack of it) of policies and programs in delivering promised results. We, too, in our earlier publications have praised the conventional wisdom of large monitoring and evaluation systems built to measure the actions of a national government or even a sector within government. We now know that these systems are not useful in many developing countries. In addition to needing the commitment of leaders, sustainable donor funding, expertise in data collection and analysis across the entire government, and civil servants who are held accountable for delivering quality services, large M&E systems often do not produce information in time for decision makers to solve immediate problems.

New mobile technologies, however, can be used to rapidly feed back information about specific services—where citizens' expectations are not being met and where they can be improved, where services are working and where they are not. Another drawback of the conventional M&E model is that information is held tightly within a small group in government and rarely widely communicated back to citizens or to individual service providers. Widely available performance information provides an opportunity to learn as you go. When citizens, providers, decision makers, and other stakeholders have the same information at the same time, more ideas can be generated, learning can be widespread, and opportunities for experimentation can flourish.

Unfortunately, two elements in short supply in many countries, including in South Asia, are trustworthy data and committed champions willing to use information for decision making. Even so, we can point to a number of examples where government officials have led the way in making sure that data have driven decision making. For example, the government of India embarked on a significant effort to reduce its HIV and AIDS epidemic through

Box 2.6

HIV Control in India

Soon after the first HIV/AIDS cases emerged in 1986, the government of India established the National AIDS Committee in the Ministry of Health and Welfare, which in turn designed and launched the National AIDS Control Organization (NACO). NACO was charged with monitoring the infection rates among populations most likely to spread the disease, such as sex workers in urban areas. Data from continuous monitoring allowed the government of India to design and implement targeted programs to mitigate the problem.

First, the government learned that the epidemic was primarily restricted to the southern and northeastern regions of the country. As a result of diligent monitoring and new knowledge about where the greatest increase in new infections was occurring, key programs were designed to prevent the epidemic from spreading. The programs included increasing knowledge among low-literacy and labor populations and increasing condom use among those visiting commercial sex workers and those involved with intravenous drug use. The program was expanded at the state level to focus on monitoring infection rates among high-risk groups. Michel Sidibe, executive director of the UN AIDS program, often spoke about how India's successful program began with an evidence-informed and human rights–based approach that is backed and sustained by political leadership and civil society engagement.

Source: David Wilson, Program Manager HIV and AIDS, World Bank, pers. comm.

interventions targeted at its most vulnerable populations and a commitment to monitor infections with trustworthy data. As a result, India saw a historic 50 percent decline in the number of new HIV infections in just one decade (box 2.6).

Even Good Information Is Not a Substitute for Sustained and Committed Leadership

Much has been said about how patronage- and clientele-based political and administrative systems would stifle or game any attempt to change public administration systems from "goodies for the few" to "services for all." Yet the dynamic generated by freedom of information, rapid flows of credible data within and outside organizations, and social media must eventually transform leadership and enhance accountability. Information monopolies have driven the inability or unwillingness of political and administrative leaders to "do the right thing." With that excuse removed and citizens demanding services, a shift is bound to occur in the often-ossified bureaucracies of emerging economies. When political leaders armed with quality data emerge and start demanding performance from their administrations, and when those politicians show staying power, internal resistance in bureaucracies will start crumbling. It takes time to change laws that protect public servants from dismissal, but the writing will be on the wall. It is no surprise that leaders such as the chief minister of Punjab, Shahbaz Sharif, the chief minister of Madhya Pradesh, Shivraj Singh, the governor of Minas Gerais state, Neves da Cunha, or the Indonesia minister of finance, Sri Mulyani Indrawati, came to their posts on platforms of public sector performance and transparency.

Two decades ago that would have been unlikely or impossible, as few leaders, particularly in developing countries, were focusing on using information to improve service delivery. The expectations that many of the tools raised were premature. To put to use the tools that can support performance improvement, leadership is required. Training of managers and staff is needed. Change also demands a fundamental shift from a compliance to an improvement mindset (Hanna 2010).

Digital Information Is Giving Citizens and Government New Power

Digital-era public sector models are replacing 1980s-to-1990s-era reforms (Dunleavy et al. 2008; Hanna 2010). Technology is enabling new forms of democratic input and citizen feedback (Hanna 2010). Dave Eggers explained it well when he said, "Today's technology can play a crucial role in fixing the problems of modern government, changing how we get to work, how we pay our taxes, how we register our business, and how our kids learn" (Eggers 2005).

Mobile phones and related technologies are the starting point. If well applied, technology can change the relations between citizens and their elected officials, and more important, those between leaders and administrations. Social media can be used to spread the word and push change. Arif Ahmad Khan could not trust his own inspectors to tell him whether or not his water filtration system was performing. In such a case, even if a manager is aware of a problem, he has neither the information to understand its exact nature (because information asymmetry protects field-level staff from discovery) nor the tools to interact effectively with those who can fix it. Neither does he have direct access to the clients who can tell him whether what his staff tells him is correct. This has been the age-old conundrum in public management—until now. Digital technology, made cheaply and widely available to governments, may enable inspectors armed with smartphones to document a performance problem within hours. Don't want to rely on inspectors because they may not report on the full range of issues? No worries! Call the beneficiaries and find out how things are going. Surely they would not be conservative with the truth. The South Asian countries that we have looked at are using digital technology to solve immediate problems, such as the fight against dengue fever, and to wage longer-term battles with petty corruption.

Digital Information Technology Needs Leadership to Become Smart Government

Like any government reforms, innovations in information technology also need leadership and entrepreneurialism to have real impact (box 2.7). "It takes visionary leadership and entrepreneurship to realize the potential opportunities for innovation and transformation. Digital technology does not substitute for leadership. Innovation is not requirements driven but opportunity driven" (Hanna 2010).

Leaders like Bill Clinton believed 20 years ago that information and communication technology would transform how government could solve problems. Communities such as Tillamook, Oregon, and hundreds of others have experimented with technology and solved one problem and then moved on to apply the new method to new settings and other problems. One could argue that solving problems one-by-one does not a transformation make. But the lessons of Billy Hamilton, vice chancellor of the Texas A&M University System, who designed the Texas Performance Review back in 1993, are instructive. Billy encouraged Texas state agencies to identify promising practices from around the world and select ideas that

Box 2.7

Leading Reforms in Rwanda from the Top

With a commitment to scale up the treatment of HIV/AIDS, in 2004 Rwanda introduced the first national mobile- and Internet-based reporting system in Africa to monitor the rapid expansion of the treatment program. Minister of Health Agnes Binagwaho[a] and her colleagues saw the potential of an electronic system that could monitor key indicators and support their plan to expand treatment nationwide. The resulting system, named TRACnet, built on the rapidly expanding mobile network that was being built in Rwanda in the same period. TRACnet, having now successfully operated for a decade, is unique in Africa and is the earliest and longest-running example of such a monitoring system in this book.

Each month, clinical providers in facilities report data on the number of patients under treatment by age, gender, and stage of disease into the TRACnet system. Of the providers 14 percent used the Internet to enter their data into a bilingual website (French and English) and 86 percent used their mobile phones to call a dedicated, toll-free phone number and respond to a voice survey, entering the data using the keypad. Data from every treatment facility nationwide were instantly available on a dashboard, enabling district and national officials to closely monitor and manage the program as it expanded from reaching just 15 percent of eligible patients in 2005 to 79 percent by 2010.

In a 2011 review of the system, a number of benefits were documented.[b] TRACnet technology facilitated standardized data collection and analysis and has improved data management systems, which became quick and easy, even for the most remote health facilities. Improving information exchange between health facilities and the national level has reinforced the accountability of HIV services and health facilities. The system has helped to overcome some and has the potential to address other key challenges in health information systems for resource-limited settings, including late reports, incomplete data, and lack of feedback from the central level to peripheral levels. The TRACnet system has enhanced the quantity of information obtained from health facilities and has facilitated its use to inform the national program. For instance, TRACnet data are utilized by the national program in ART quantification and procurement, making the system quite valuable for HIV decision makers.

Although TRACnet was introduced as a monitoring system, Rwanda decided to build on it to address other problem areas.

- In 2010, Rwanda was expanding treatment to HIV positive infants and decided to build on TRACnet to accelerate reporting of lab results from the national laboratory back to clinics. Using blinded SMS messages to transmit the results, turnaround time was cut from an average of 90 days to five days. The use of this mobile system, together with other steps, has contributed to a significant reduction in the time it is taking to initiate treatment of affected infants with life-saving drugs.

(Continued)

Box 2.7 *(Continued)*

- In 2012, a real-time stock-out reporting system was added to help ensure the continuity of supply of the drugs needed for treatment of AIDS. As of September 2013, 255 shortages and 158 stock-outs in ARVs were reported through TRACnet—allowing district and national officials to manage the situations quickly in order to prevent drug interruptions among HIV/AIDS patients.

- In 2013, Rwanda adapted the system and introduced the first national electronic disease surveillance system in Africa. As of 2014, health officers in all health facilities, including 502 sites across all 30 districts in Rwanda that provide drugs for AIDS, are reporting every week and reporting suspected outbreaks in real time. TRACnet replaced a paper-based disease surveillance system characterized by late and incomplete reporting and consequent difficulty in identifying and responding to outbreaks rapidly so as to limit their spread and fatality. The new electronic system has turned this situation around. As of March 2014, 98 percent of facilities are reporting on time and 99.1 percent of reports are complete, helping officials detect outbreaks rapidly, investigate them, and mount a quick response within the country and across the borders.

Notes

a. Today, Minister Binagwaho continues to champion the use of innovative technology to strengthen Rwanda's health system. The *Guardian* recently named her one of the top 10 global development tweeters to watch in 2014 for her updates on health in Rwanda.

b. S. Nsanzimana, R. Hinda, D. W. Lowrance, S. Cishahayo, J. P. Nyemazi, R. Muhayimpundu, C. Karema, P. L. Raghunathan, A. Binagwaho, and D. J. Riedel, "Cell Phone- and Internet-Based Monitoring and Evaluation of the National Antiretroviral Treatment Program during Rapid Scale-up in Rwanda: TRACnet, 2004–2010," *JAIDS* 59, no.2 (2011): e17–e23.

---

held promise if tailored to the local environment. The State of Texas became known not only in the United States but around the world as a public sector reform model. Today's governments would be wise to encourage the "let a thousand flowers bloom" reform strategy, while continuing to advance earlier public management reforms that have worked in specific settings. Billy Hamilton did not stop his ongoing programs of longer-term fiscal reforms while pursuing innovative experiments. He moved forward on both strategies. It cannot be emphasized enough that in many developing countries it is important to continue to invest in a strong public management system and the people whose job it is to perform within it. Strong accountability systems and honest leaders who encourage innovation and who stay the course are critical to making use of new 21st-century tools. Specific reforms, such as pay reform, can improve incentives for public servants to carry out their duties and encourage them to learn new tasks necessary in the age of digital or smart government.

Undeniable Improvements in South Asia

Service delivery is improving in a number of South Asian countries. For example, Pakistan's Punjab Citizen Feedback Model is harnessing the power of call centers, text messages, and personal phone calls to rebuild the community's trust by soliciting feedback from citizens receiving pensions, prenatal health care, and property registration services. That effort was initially called the "Jhang model" because it was conceived when one of the authors served as the district coordination officer in Jhang in 2008. Today, the effort is being extended by the Punjab Chief Minister's Secretariat across the entire province of 90 million people.

The model works as follows: Imagine that you, the citizen, go to a government office to obtain a service—let's say to obtain a driver's license. The official records your mobile number, along with other details of the transaction. The data are passed on to local call officers and to a call center, through an online data entry form or simply via an SMS message. Later, you are called by one of those local officers, or you receive a text message, in which you are asked about your experience getting your driving license. Was it just okay? Fantastic? Or were you dissatisfied with the service you received or the treatment you encountered? The local officers are calling a few of those who received services, but the call centers are calling thousands of service beneficiaries.

Citizens are excited. "Respected Sir, your message transported to an imaginary land and filled me with delight and jubilation on the check and balance introduced by the government. Nothing like [it] has happened with me before," a citizen named Bilal Ahmad wrote on April 15, 2011, in response to a message from an officer asking him if he experienced corruption when he registered his property transaction with the revenue department. Some citizens report corruption. The feedback collected through calls or the SMS is reviewed, and patterns are identified. If many complaints are reported against a particular official, he or his supervisor is counseled, censured, or even punished.

This model is applicable in a wide variety of service delivery settings. District coordination officer Ahmad Ali Kamboh said,

"For district rural health centers, it was difficult for health officers to supervise and monitor service delivery. Using this system, I can analyze the performance, the ratio of deliveries, and efficiency. I've initiated actions against several officials based on this feedback" (Siddiqi 2011).

As of April 11, 2014, more than 4 million citizens of Pakistan had been contacted and surveyed about their transactions with the departments of revenue, health, and education, and their responses entered into the system. The innovation of this program is that it does not wait for complaints to be lodged. Rather, service beneficiaries are identified and contacted on a large scale to seek feedback and analyze systemic problems in service performance, so they can be fixed and citizens can receive better services.

Mobile phones are not the only technology achieving massive scale in South Asia. Another is the user identification system. Given the ever-present bad news about Pakistan, it is hard to imagine that Pakistan boasts a best practice biometric national identity registration system. Created in 2001, the National Database Registration Authority (NADRA) has registered some 91 million citizens, roughly 96 percent of the population. The impact has been massive. In the last election, the NADRA database was used as the basis of electoral rolls, cleaning up massively the overpopulated lists of yesteryear that underlay the persistent return to office of entrenched politicians. When NADRA announced a service with the Election Commission of Pakistan by which any citizen could query the location of their vote by sending in their National Identity Number (NIC), 50,000 voters verified their entries on the preliminary electoral rolls within half an hour. The cleaner-than-usual election, among other factors, is credited with making possible the strong showing of the Pakistan Justice Movement.

Over time, NADRA has begun working with a range of departments because of the utility of its data. During disasters, the NADRA database was used to verify people's identities and distribute relief grants to them. NADRA has also been using the database to identify bodies of victims of suicide bombings and other such tragic events. More recently, NADRA's database management has allowed the establishment of the Benazir Income Support Program. A nationwide survey was conducted to assign poverty scores to each household in Pakistan. The survey results, in combination with the NADRA database, allowed 7 million of the country's poorest households to be identified for delivery of cash grants. Numerous other examples, for crime control, banking, citizen services, bill payments, and so forth, are under way.

Box 2.8
The Lahore Waste Management Company

The estimated 9 million inhabitants of Lahore, the second-biggest city in Pakistan and the capital of the Punjab province, annually produce an estimated 500 tons of solid waste. The solid waste management wing of the city government maintained a force of around 10,000 workers to sweep the roads and streets and a fleet of 500 vehicles to collect waste. Nevertheless, Lahore was a visibly dirty city. Moreover, corruption and mismanagement were rampant. Sanitary workers remained busy with private jobs while sharing their government salaries with their supervisors. Drivers were known to steal a substantial percentage of vehicle fuel because no mechanism existed to monitor their waste collection routines.

Frustrated with the lack of progress, Shahbaz Sharif, the chief minister of the province, handed over the waste management function in 2010 to the Lahore Waste Management Company (LWMC), an autonomous, government-owned company. He also provided the requisite financial resources.

After taking over, LWMC identified three main flaws. First, no tool was available to monitor the company's operations—to check if vehicles are going out, whether the manual sweeping workers were on the job, and so forth. Second, there was no way to measure the amount of waste being transported to the dump to estimate collection efficiency. And finally, there was no way to learn how satisfied citizens were with LWMC's performance and what problems they faced.

Each of the problems was solved using digital technology. Tracking devices were installed in all LWMC vehicles, and each vehicle was assigned a route and containers that it had to collect waste from daily. Waste collection vehicles were also weighed, using an automated system, before and after trips to calculate the amount of waste they were collecting in a tamper-free manner. And once data started coming in, digital tools were used to optimize the drivers' routes for maximum efficiency. The activities of the drivers were tracked live, and fuel was assigned based on distance traveled. The LWMC aggressively promoted a complaint management system managed by a third-party call center. Any complaints are pursued actively, and unresolved complaints are tracked rigorously.

In 2012, the bulk of LWMC operations were handed over to two private contractors. LWMC's management responsibilities were reduced considerably, but it continued to focus on monitoring. "Now we are simply monitoring to ensure that the contractor is delivering what was committed," explained the CEO of the company. The contractors have regularized shifts to eight-hour periods, and more workers have

(Continued)

Box 2.8 *(Continued)*

been employed in areas where manpower was consistently short. The gratuity of 1,200 to 1,500 rupees that workers previously had to pay supervisors in an ecosystem of corruption has also gradually been eliminated by removal of corrupt supervisors. "Attendance figures for our workers have now reached 90 percent in some areas of Lahore, which is a big milestone for us. When we established the attendance monitoring system and started recording attendance, the figure was around 60 percent to 65 percent, and in some union councils was even as low as 60 percent," he said.

Smartphones were also put to work to add another layer of checking. Assistant managers conduct random attendance checks, facilitate complaint resolution, or manage large-scale operations such as cleaning plots as needed, and record their activities by taking GPS-tagged photos that appear on a live dashboard at the LWMC office. "Once they take these geo-tagged pictures I know they are doing their job and they are doing so on-site," the CEO explained.

Better resource allocation and reducing leakage are also clearly noticeable. "When we started operating the company, we had 500 vehicles in our fleet and were issuing 14,000 liters of fuel per day. But after launching the tracking system, optimizing all routes, and starting a system where fuel was issued on the basis of the amount of work the drivers are doing, the fuel allocation came down to almost 9,000 liters per day."

LWMC managers had noticed that even when their vehicles' capacity was 2.5 tons, drivers would often bring as little as 600 kilograms of waste in per trip. Scanners now record and report the weight of trucks entering the dump site. Managers spent considerable time explaining to the drivers that the amount of waste they bring to the dump is as important as the number of trips they make. As a result of the effort, waste collection efficiency in Lahore increased from a dismal 50 percent two years ago to between 80 percent and 90 percent today, and in some seasons has even gone up to 100 percent. Internationally it is estimated that when the collection efficiency of a city crosses 80 percent, the city starts appearing clean.

Source: Author communications with Lahore Waste Management Company.

Across the border in India, the Indian Aadhar, run by the Unique Identification Authority of India (UIDAI), is an even larger effort to issue a unique, biometric-based identity number to every resident. The identity card contains a unique 12-digit number, known as the Aadhar number, and is linked to demographics and biometrics of each person, such as photographs, fingerprints, and so forth. Aadhar eliminates the duplicate and fake identities in several government and private databases. Nandan Nilekani, the entrepreneur and force behind Aadhar, believes that it would be the basic building block for any welfare service, financial inclusion scheme, or other targeted program that the government may want to launch. People could be authenticated online, and their receipt of a service can be recorded in the cloud. That means that citizens can obtain self-service on the Internet or using their mobile phones. "Suddenly they are empowered because now they have the choice of accessing their public service anywhere in India" (interview with McKinsey and Company, October 2012). Bangladesh is also building a biometric citizen identification and registration system.

Privacy Concerns Are Real

We share these stories with our eyes wide open to current debate over privacy concerns. Having one's most personal information incorporated into big data systems that are shared widely across the government, outside the government, and even outside one's country is a recipe for possible misuse by nefarious agents, including those stealing our identities for financial gain, or even by the police for unlawful gain of private information. The United States recently ruled that no mobile phone can be taken by police without a proper search warrant signed by a judge, and India's Supreme Court restrained the Centre and the Unique Identification Authority of India from sharing the vast biometric database with any third party or agency without the consent of the registered person. Moreover, the Court ruled that no information will be released to a third party—government or private—unless the cardholder consents. And in concert with the U.S. rule, the India Supreme Court made explicit privacy protections during criminal investigations (*Nation*, March 25, 2014, New Delhi).

As the middle class grows, so will privacy concerns.

Still, when discussing privacy issues with Pakistani and Indian colleagues and friends we learned that at this time, privacy concerns do not seem to be as important to the average citizen as having the access to government welfare services that an identity number provides. As the middle class grows across the region, however, and as more and more people enroll in Aadhar, we fully expect that privacy issues will grow as a critical concern to citizens over the level of openness of their most private information, regardless of the benefits of doing so.

Communication Technologies Open New Doors

What do these communication technologies mean for improving government? Basic phones, smartphones, and digital maps create three astonishing new possibilities. First, the quality, level of detail, and timeliness of data have improved radically, consisting not just of the old, easily fudged numbers, but also of photos, locations, audios, and videos. This addresses the well-known thorny challenge of measurement of the inputs and the outputs. Second, vast numbers of beneficiaries of any service can be contacted via text messages, automated calls, and call centers, and can be selected on the basis of any sectoral or spatial characteristic, to inquire about the quality of any service. This addresses the critical challenges of measuring outcomes and communicating state intent to beneficiaries. Third, the visualization of specific information—on digital maps, in social media space, and through related digital means—permits it to be communicated to internal and external audiences relatively easily. This addresses the central challenge of management access to data and beneficiary participation. An unlimited number of government applications can be built with any combination of these enabling technologies.

Most governments have been setting up computer kiosks to create access for rural populations. The presence of a computer in literally every village, or even every household, will create a very large architecture for delivering other governance services. Possibly the biggest impact of smartphones will come when they enable seamless access to the enormous biometric identity databases that South Asia has been busy building over the last 10 years to enable delivery of services in remote locations. Does all this sound a bit unattainable for a region where only recently a young journalist friend was nearly assassinated for his modern views on engagement with the West and the outside world and his use of the mass electronic media to express his views? One hopes that these contradictory events in the region will not impede its ability to take advantage of positive global reform trends.

References

Andrews, M., L. Pritchett, and M. Woolcock. 2012. "Escaping Capability Traps through Problem-Driven Iterative Adaptation (PDIA)." Working Paper 299, Center for Global Development, Washington, DC.

Banerjee, A., R. Glennester, and E. Duflo. 2008. "Putting a Band-Aid on a Corpse: Incentives for Nurses in the Indian Public Health Care System." *Journal of the European Economic Association* 6: 2–3.

Callen, M., S. Gulzar, A. Hasanain, and Y. Khan. 2013. "The Political Economy of Public Employee Absence, Experimental Evidence from Pakistan." Paper, International Growth Centre, Pakistan.

Chaudhury, N., J. Hammer, M. Kremer, K. Muralidharan, and H. F. Rogers. 2006. "Missing in Action: Teacher and Health Worker Absence in Developing Countries." *Journal of Economic Perspectives* 20 (1): 91–116.

DeRenzi, B., L. Findlater, J. Payne, B. Birnbau, J. Mangilima, T. Parisk, G. Borriello, and N. Lesh. 2012. "Improving Community Health Worker Performance through Automated SMS." ICTD '12. Proceedings of the Fifth International Conference on Information and Communication Technologies and Development, March 12–15, Atlanta, GA, USA.

Dunleavy, P., H. Margetts, S. Bastow, and J. Tinkler. 2008. *Digital Era Governance: IT Corporations, the State and e-Government*. Rev. ed. Oxford: Oxford University Press.

Eggers, David. 2005. *Government 2.0: Using Technology to Improve Education, Cut Red Tape, Reduce Gridlock, and Enhance Democracy*. Lanham, MD: Rowman and Littlefield.

Gorgens, M., and J. Kusek. 2010. *Making Monitoring and Evaluation Systems Work*. Washington, DC: World Bank.

Government of Pakistan. 2014. *Social and Living Standards Measurement Survey*. Statistics Division, Islamabad.

Hanna, Nagy K. 2010. *Transforming Government and Building the Information Society*. New York: Springer Publishing.

In the Public Interest. 2014. "Privatization Myths Debunked." Accessed February 20, 2014. http://www.inthepublicinterest.org/node/457.

Kettl, D. 2005. *The Global Public Management Revolution*. 2nd ed. Washington, DC: Brookings Institution Press.

Kusek, J., and R. Rist. 2004. *Ten Steps to a Results Based Monitoring and Evaluation System*. Washington, DC: World Bank.

Larbi, G. A. 1999. *Public Sector Reforms and Crisis-Ridden States*. United Nations Research Institute for Social Development (UNRISD), ISSNL 1012- 6511, Geneva.

Manning, N., and J. Watkins. 2013. "Targeting Results, Diagnosing the Means: Innovative Approaches for Improving Public Sector Delivery." World Bank, GET Notes.

Osborne, D., and T. Gaebler. 1992. *Reinventing Government*. New York: Penguin.

Schaffer, R. H., and R. N. Ashkenas. 2005. *Rapid Results*. San Francisco: Jossey Bass.

Schick, A. 2003. "The Performing State, Reflection on an Idea Whose Time Has Come, but Whose Implementation Has Not." *OECD Journal on Budgeting*. 3: 2.

———. 1998. "Why Most Developing Countries Should Not Try New Zealand's Reforms." *World Bank Research Observer* 13 (1): 123–31.

Siddiqi, K. 2011. "Proactive Governance." *Friday Times* (Pakistan), July 1–7. Accessed June 14, 2014. http://www.thefridaytimes.com/beta2/tft/article.php?issue=20110701&page=8.

Verheijen, T., and D. Coombes, eds. 1998. *Innovations in Public Management: Experiences from East and West Europe*. Cheltenham, U.K.: Edward Elgar.

Walton, M., S. Devarajan, and S. Khemani. 2011. "Civil Society, Public Action and Accountability in Africa." Policy Research Working Paper 5733, World Bank, Washington, DC.

World Bank. 2012. "Equity in Public Service Delivery in Tanzania and Uganda." Policy Note Report No. 74355, World Bank, Washington, DC.

———. 2013. "Review and Research Agenda on Results-Based Management in Brazilian States." Policy Note Report No. 82592-BR, World Bank, Washington, DC.

Chapter 3
Solutions

There are 4 billion cell phones in use today. Many of them are in the hands of market vendors, rickshaw drivers and others who've historically lacked access to education and opportunity. Information networks have become a great leveler and we should use them.

—Hillary Clinton

Javed Mahmood, the chief secretary of the provincial government of Punjab, Pakistan, sat for hours a day outside his office for several weeks during 2008 to receive complaints from citizens. "Accessibility is the most important thing. Enabling easy access is half the job done," Mahmood always advised his staff (pers. comm.).

Mahmood, leading the nearly one-million-strong civil service of the largest province in Pakistan, with over 50 percent of the country's population, understood the importance of reaching out to citizens. Likewise, across the world, senior civil servants, as well as politicians, have always used direct engagement with citizens to show that they understand their concerns. But whereas meeting with constituents is necessary when candidates are campaigning for election, direct engagement is not the answer for effective governance. What makes human interest news stories is not always relevant to citizen welfare. Government officials are expected to govern tens of thousands of citizens and solve serious systemic problems affecting them.

Petty corruption, for example, is an issue that touches most South Asians, and not surprisingly, the middle-class voter. Many countries have put in place dedicated and nonpolitical bodies—often called an ombudsman, a complaint cell, or something else—that citizens can contact by phone or mail to register complaints. Results as to whether the complaints get resolved or not are at best mixed. In a typical case, in Khyber Pakhtunkhwa, Pakistan, the chief minister,

Pervez Khattak, soon after coming to power in mid 2013, set up a complaint cell "to eliminate corruption, injustice, inequality, and antisocial elements." He promised that if "the complaint is genuine, not biased and correct" the government will act and provide justice to the complainants. Eight months after its establishment, the cell had received 13,959 complaints. However, only 2,000-plus complaints were able to be "redressed." More than 10,000 were investigated and thrown out because of a lack of information or legitimacy. "Some 70 percent of 'complaints' received do not have actionable information" (http://crckp.gov.pk/). In Delhi in early 2004, an anticorruption hotline was a flagship effort promoted heavily by the Common Man Party, which ran on an anticorruption platform and surprised everyone in India when it won 40 percent of the seats in the 2013 state elections. Unfortunately, the anticorruption effort was quietly discontinued because it was not delivering results. The number of calls the hotline received was huge, but the vast majority of them were not related to corruption or bribery.

Trying to distinguish legitimate complaints among a flood of them is not easy, nor is it a new problem. Several centuries ago, the omnipotent Mughal emperors in Delhi struggled with the same challenges. The Italian writer and traveler Niccolao Manucci, who worked in the Mughal court, was recorded as saying that the Mughal empire "was overrun with men whose only profession is to act as false witnesses or to forge signatures."

Emperor Akbar, Secretary Mahmood, Minister Khattak, and the Common Man Party, although separated by centuries, had similar concerns about reaching citizens with real problems needing immediate solutions. Compared with his successors, Akbar faced a huge disadvantage. If he wanted to know how satisfied citizens were with his administration, he needed to reach out to them face to face. Today tens of millions of citizens—not just a few thousand, as with the Khyber Pakhtunkhwa province complaint cell or with the Common Man Party hotline, or the hundreds reached by the zealous Mahmood—can be reached. We mean "proactively reached"—government finds them, and not the other way around.

We mean "proactively reached"—government finds them, and not the other way around.

A Model for Change

When policy makers proactively reach citizens, they cut out the multiple layers of red tape and often inaction from middle managers or other intermediaries. Also, when the government is the one reaching out to citizens and not the other way around, there is opportunity to collect a wider range of opinions or feedback. We know that citizens expect their government to deliver quality services. In other words, they expect their government to work! When governments do not work, citizens don't always care why—they only want to know when. When will the garbage be picked up? When will the trains be running again? When will the streets be safe to walk at night?

Governments also want to know what is working on their watch. Arif Ahmad Khan, whose experience with oversight of water filtration plants in Sindh province was discussed in chapter 2, certainly wished he had known that those plants were not meeting service expectations before he had to be told so by the chief minister. With mobile technology, government and citizens do not have to wait weeks or months for answers about how their government is performing. Daily follow-up at low cost is becoming possible, even in the most disadvantaged parts of the world.

With mobile technology, government and citizens do not have to wait weeks or months for answers about how their government is performing. Daily follow-up at low cost is becoming possible, even in the most disadvantaged parts of the world.

Mike Trucano, a World Bank expert in using information and communication technology in the education sector, has written extensively about the use of mobile phones for large-scale data collection in even the poorest and most remote countries. The phones have dramatically reduced the time government officials need to make informed decisions (pers. comm.).

The authors ask: Why, against such great odds, are we beginning to see more open and accountable government in parts of South Asia? We wondered if the region's high acceptance of mobile technology might be a factor in enabling it to exploit the five global shifts discussed earlier. In researching these questions, we reviewed approximately 200 mobile technology innovations. We examined both successful and failed efforts in the United States, East Asia, Europe, and South Asia. Specifically, we identified efforts where mobile technology allowed government to leapfrog older, more conventional government reforms. Among the many efforts we reviewed, we noticed that the ones gaining a foothold in South Asia share similar approaches in the ways they introduced various aspects of mobile phone technology. Many related to improving one-way messaging from the government to citizen, such as sending information to pregnant women in Bangladesh about prenatal needs, or sending broadcast messages alerting citizens to natural events such as flooding or cyclones. A smaller number introduced two-way communication schemes, such as sending messages to citizens to solicit data for one purpose or another, as in the Proactive Feedback model in Punjab. Other reforms applied GPS/GIS-enabled smartphone technology to new ways of doing business, such as improved crime solving or dispatching services where they were most needed. Moreover, the important role of champions and leaders to support and nudge the effort along was underscored across all the reforms that seemed to take hold. In fact, the foothold reforms seemed to be categorized according to five solutions:

1. Seeking proactive feedback from identified beneficiaries
2. Collecting performance information from the point of delivery in real time
3. Using common dashboards to communicate performance
4. Nudging champions from above
5. Experimenting with several innovations simultaneously

Five Solutions for Smart Reforms

Solution 1. Seeking proactive feedback from identified beneficiaries. Talk about citizen feedback and communication technologies with a government official, and the conversation often turns to the topics of hotlines, complaint cells, and various passive e-mail or text-message-based tools for receiving complaints. These grievance redress mechanisms have drawbacks that limit their usefulness as feedback tools. The biggest problem: the squeakiest wheel typically gets the most grease, regardless of its importance or priority within government. In addition, the administrative costs of inquiring into every complaint to determine whether it is valid or not can be high. Just as a letter to the editor is not a reliable barometer of citizens' views, one complaint cannot be considered the voice of the community.

An organized, proactive system to obtain evaluative information from identified beneficiaries is quite different from the usual complaint or anticorruption hotlines, which tend to focus only on negative information and individual redress. Is reaching out to beneficiaries to inquire about the quality of services received for systems reform an impossible challenge? Not at all. The private sector initiates contacts with its customers continually to get their opinions about services rendered. Who among us has not been contacted by a hotel we have stayed in seeking our opinion on the quality of service? Why shouldn't the public sector proactively

The private sector initiates contacts with its customers continually to get their opinions about services rendered.

seek customer (that is, citizen) feedback? Why rely exclusively on complaints and deem that sufficient for citizen engagement?

To be fair, the public sector could not engage in the proactive collection of feedback from citizens until only a few years ago. It is hard to believe that a mere decade ago, the only people with landlines were the middle or upper classes in most South Asian countries. Text messaging had yet to become the dominant form of communication among the young. Letter-based surveys were probably never attempted on a large scale because of the cost and limited applicability to the lower-middle classes and the poor. In 2014 even those in the lowest income brackets in South Asia are actively participating in the cell phone revolution, making direct engagement with them possible.

Since 2012, the Citizen Feedback model in Punjab has proactively engaged citizens across a dozen services, including police and the land revenue, urban development, and health departments. The citizen feedback or proactive feedback model is a system in which data are collected and categorized daily, serving as a permanent survey and providing both a snapshot and a continuous stream of information about services throughout a province, a district, a subdistrict, or other local jurisdiction. The data help identify patterns and trends in the performance of departments and services. If a particular facility consistently receives unsatisfactory marks from citizens, then managers can concentrate on that facility. This is especially useful in attacking petty corruption. Whereas one citizen complaint about having to give a bribe could be fabricated, when one office or official is consistently being incriminated for corruption by a range of citizens, that is a good basis for disciplinary action against the official or for asking their supervisor to explain the lax supervision. By May 2014, district officials had reported written evidence of more than 4,000 corrective actions into the dashboard (Saif 2014).

The program offers several benefits. It can be rolled out quickly and set up for a wide number of services in which petty corruption is rife. The model can be expanded to monitor quality of service delivery. Limited literacy can be addressed by sending citizens SMS messages in the local dialect and by having workers telephone beneficiaries. As we have stated, it is in effect a permanent survey seeking information from users of services. It prepares a live, electronic report card for every facility, as responses are associated with the facility that reported the cell number. Most important, it communicates state responsiveness to citizens. The Punjab program is spreading across Pakistan, and two additional provinces, Khyber Pakhtunkhwa and Sindh, are now applying it for various provincial services.

Despite the Citizen Feedback model's immediate benefits, challenges remain. In some areas it cannot locate accurate or complete information. A cheating taxpayer, for example, is not likely to report dishonest tax inspectors if they have worked together to rob the state. It does not work with citizen-to-citizen disputes. Moreover, citizens may feel powerless, may fear to assert themselves, or may not even be aware of the required quality of service.

Nevertheless, proactive citizen engagement is an important component of the innovations that are working in South Asia. Details may differ, but it seems that this approach of citizen engagement can be transported to many different development contexts. Consider a school located in a remote place, for example. Conventional reforms have been introducing mechanisms to receive parent complaints for some time. A proactive system, such as the one practiced by the education department in Punjab, Pakistan, would involve collecting the cell numbers of the parents and school council members to ask them their opinions about the quality of education in their school. Securing cell numbers is also a way to share other information using an SMS or to inquire about other services, such as sanitation or health.

Proactive Engagement with Communities to Monitor Hand Pump Maintenance in Bihar

In Bihar, an overwhelming part of the rural population depends on hand pumps to obtain safe drinking water. The Public Health Department (PHED), which installs and maintains the hand pumps, finds it difficult to track their use and maintenance. The number of hand pumps actually serviced or replaced may even be less than what the field staff report through departmental channels.

In Nalanda district, mobile phones are being used to monitor drinking water infrastructure and service to more than 15,500 households across 105 villages of Rajgir Block. In addition to using smartphones to mark the location of each hand pump, the PHED tags the households that use a specific pump. A short message service (SMS) sends periodic SMS messages to community members asking about the working status of the hand pump. If the SMS response from the community reports that the pump is faulty, the automated scheduler sends an SMS alert to the PHED repair team to service it. When it completes repairs, the team remotely updates the functional status of the hand pump by sending a message to the central server. The repair team's update of the hand pump's status in the central database initiates another SMS loop to verify that the reported repair has actually been accomplished. Only when the community users send SMS messages confirming that the hand pump is working properly is the repair of the pump considered complete. Vijay Kumar Srivastava, executive engineer, PHED, affirms, "This is one of the best monitoring systems I would say for Public Health Department. Now we know how many hand pumps are working in which location, how many need special repair, and how many need minor repair. We not only can plan for repair work but also plan for new sinking of hand pumps."

Because this mobile phone–based water infrastructure monitoring provides better service to rural water users, it is proposed to be extended to all 68 revenue blocks of Bhagalpur, Nalanda, Purnia, and West Champaran districts of Bihar. The system would cover 110,000 hand pumps that serve more than 11 million people in approximately 15,000 villages. What was learned from the pilot program has also influenced the design of systems to monitor water quality to assess arsenic and fluoride contamination in 22 districts of Bihar.

Using Call Centers to Mobilize School Councils

In Kenya, researchers Duflo, Dupas, and Kremer (2007) found that when school committees made up of parents were given funds specifically to hire an extra teacher over whom the committee had direct hiring control, children's test scores improved. Moreover, improvements in scores were even greater when the school committees were specifically trained how to monitor the extra teacher and reminded that it was within their power to fire and replace her or him. In India, however, Banerjee et al. (2010) found that training village education councils had no effect on access or quality.

In theory, parental participation in school affairs should lead to improved quality everywhere. The reality in context, as seen in the two experiments, is more complicated, and introducing parental participation in public sector settings on a large scale even more so. Good ideas that succeed with NGO-run facilities in carefully controlled trials often fail because of the high cost and the political economy of the harsh public sector environment.

In March 2013, the Punjab School Education Department, encouraged by the results of the ongoing effort for proactive collection of citizen feedback, started an information and communication technology (ICT)–based school council mobilization program in 2,500 schools. Private sector agents were retained to call parents because text messages were not likely to work for illiterate or semiliterate fathers and mothers. The agents had a planned script in the local dialect, and female agents called female family members periodically to communicate information about their roles, noting their responses and encouraging them to participate in school affairs.

Compared with the standard NGO-delivered training, this innovative effort—some 80 percent of council members and households have mobile phones—incurs less cost. It provides sustained engagement over the three-year life of the council and obtains data on each council member during each conversation. A recent third-party review by the United Kingdom–based firm Cambridge Education found that some 70 percent of council members who had received the earlier training considered this delivery mode to be better. Continuous engagement also resulted in a high retention rate of the imparted messages. The schools department now aims to expand the effort to 45,000-plus public sector schools in the province.

Solution 2. Collecting performance information from the point of delivery in real time.
Checking the attendance of officials posted in remote facilities such as schools is a challenge. Monitoring the movement of inspectors, extension workers, rural health workers, and others whose jobs require travel around the country is even more difficult. Before mobile smartphones with Global Positioning System (GPS) capabilities, it was almost impossible to track whether a field worker was indeed making their required visits or even if the teacher was at school. Smartphones have shone a bright light on claims by civil servants that they were working and also on complaints that they were overworked. Take the case of health workers in Punjab's Khanewal district (box 3.1). Smartphone data showed that health monitors were making their requisite 15 visits during the first week of each month. When Farasat Iqbal, then head of the provincial health reform unit, became aware of the practice, he exclaimed, "So what do they do the rest of the month?" He immediately doubled the number of field inspections required each month to 30.

Box 3.1
Karnataka Beneficiary Verification System

To improve health service delivery in Karnataka, India, a pilot beneficiary verification system (BVS) was undertaken in February 2011 in two districts to verify delivery of services directly from the beneficiaries. The women enrolled were provided a "smart card" the first time they used the health service and then tracked to ensure that they obtained maternal and child health care. Feedback was obtained to verify data collected by the health care staff (Madon 2014).

The BVS systematically addressed each stage of health care service delivery through the use of handheld devices with multiple features. The devices allow the option of using magnetic swipe cards and fingerprinting for beneficiary authentication. Information on the state of health care facilities is collected using external cameras, and similar technologies are used to monitor attendance of junior health assistants. Beneficiary feedback is collected using technologies that allow voice input as an external monitoring mechanism—thereby creating a system in which, instead of the service provider claiming that a service was provided, the beneficiary verifies it, saying she has received it. The system includes tracking when a beneficiary was supposed to get checkups with alarms generated by the system automatically when a checkup was missed. Finally, all data collected through these sources is compiled in real time in a dashboard, which automatically generates reports and provides summaries of key performance indicators.

The use of portable devices and modern technology allowed the BVS system to provide a steady source of reliable data on both performance outcomes and staff activities. Madon (2014) concluded, "Data that serve to authenticate beneficiaries, identify delivery or nondelivery of services, document the status of health facilities, and obtain feedback from beneficiaries provide crucial support for health planning and resource allocation."

In the same province, smartphone monitoring of agriculture extension workers substantiated their claims that they were overburdened with other assignments throughout the year, which distracted them from their main responsibilities of helping farmers at their own farms with agriculture problems. "We work on Saturdays and Sundays and do all sorts of things. We even regulate market prices of fodder for cattle, tent prices, and other things such as where the fodder is being sold, and so forth," explained one agriculture extension field worker.

Verifying Construction Activities in Afghanistan

Monitoring the construction of small-scale community infrastructure across the length and breadth of war-torn Afghanistan, an

> **Box 3.2**
> ## Geo-Informatics for Ensuring Forest Rights in Maharashtra
>
> The Indian Forest Rights Act of 2006 granted eligible claimants of scheduled tribes and other traditional forest dwellers habitation and cultivation rights if they possessed forestland till December 13, 2005. Given the standard public administration challenges of corruption and low capacity, gathering and verifying evidence of land cultivation on or before the cutoff date and accurately measuring land parcels would be difficult, however. Some were claiming rights to forestland after the cutoff date. The government of Maharashtra overcame many of the challenges using a mobile, GPS-based geo-informatics system.
>
> A village-level committee prepares a case file containing all the information related to each claimant request. Field officials of the Forest, Revenue and Land Records Department and NGO representatives trained to measure claimant land using a GPS device, in the presence of the Forest Rights Committee (FRC), measure the claimed land and assign a unique, 13-digit alphanumeric ID to each claimant. They then submit the claim to higher-level committees. The claim is superimposed onto satellite images procured from the National Remote Sensing Agency for two time series, 2005–06 and 2007–08, and onto Google Earth images, to identify cultivated land for verification of agricultural activities prior to December 2005 (Rahman et al. 2011; Jha 2006). These images are processed using in-house software to check the validity of the claim, including analysis of elements such as chronological evidence of vegetation cover and proof of cultivation by the claimant. The measurement analysis with relevant evidence is then added to the case file for a final decision. In the words of Arvind Jha, former commissioner, Tribal Research and Training Institute (TRTI), and architect of this initiative, "We are providing the link between the villagers and the government with technical inputs that ensure smooth and accurate processing of cases and an overall robust system to implement the Forest Rights Act effectively."
>
> With such transparent, indisputable evidence for implementation of the Forest Rights Act, the government gained the trust of the tribal communities, discouraged illegal diversion of forestland, and saved large sums of money, compared to the traditional method of manual, "plane table" surveying and measuring of land.

undertaking funded by the multibillion-dollar, 33 country Afghanistan Reconstruction Trust Fund (ARTF), seems like the mother of all monitoring challenges. However, technology is aiding in the task. Third-party monitors "visit project sites with site drawings provided by counterparts, review construction quality, make suggestions for improvement, and grade quality from 1 to 5, using a number of criteria such as quality of design, materials, and workmanship" (World Bank 2014, 12). The collected location data are then located on an online map for spatial analyses. Other project-specific information is analyzed to learn about progress, problems, and next steps and to inform management decisions. These days, smartphone-based data collection mechanisms support regular, credible updates on more than 2,800 sites across the 34 provinces of the country.

The initial impetus for smartphone-based monitoring may have come from suspicions that funds were going into "ghost" schools and projects, but third-party monitoring confirmed that that was "largely a non-issue, at least for the schools monitored through the program" (World Bank 2014, 15). The bigger challenge in many cases, especially in education and in the massive National Solidarity Program, turned out to be simply management and coordination. The review explains,

> Buildings may be constructed at a slightly different location from that indicated in the plans for a number of reasons, including land availability and suitability, but the satellite imagery used in audits will show that a building does not exist on the GPS coordinates in the original plan. (World Bank 2014, 15)

In such cases, further investigation and site checks may be necessary, but once the information is available, the government can also pursue investigations and provide explanations for such discrepancies. It is important that "the TPM provides donors with a level of comfort in a governance-challenged environment" (World Bank 2014, 16). With photos and geo-tags verifying every project, clear evidence existed of where the money was being spent.

Mobile Technology to Solve Crimes Is a Global Triumph

Using information technology to solve crimes is certainly not a new concept, but in that regard New York City's Comp Stat is a global superstar. Between 1990 and 2011, homicides in New York City declined by 80 percent, robbery by 83 percent, burglary by 86 percent, and car theft by 94 percent (Rosenberg 2012). Mobile phone communication helped South Asia gain its own toehold in crime reduction. Lahore police began plotting the locations of crime incidents with smartphones and identifying the locations that showed disproportionately high criminal activity, the hot spots that needed enhanced police presence. Smartphone technology revealed hot spots for motorcycle theft at the three exit gates of a major park, where many motorcycles were parked. The police reduced theft by guarding those points more stringently and including the Lahore parking authority in efforts to prevent thefts. According to Zulfikar Hameed, the head of investigations and the force behind this effort, "The appeal of focusing limited resources on a small number of high-crime places is straightforward. If we can prevent crime at hot spot locations, then we might be able to reduce total crime," he said. "Hot spot policing is a big plank of smart policing" (*Express Tribune*, August 13, 2013, http://tribune.com.pk). The beleaguered police of Peshawar, the capital of the conflict-ridden Khyber Paktunkhwa province, are also eagerly adopting this technique.

Solution 3. Using common dashboards to communicate performance. Communication with citizens and beneficiaries about government's performance is important. Communication with beneficiaries lets them know whether actions have been taken on their feedback and sends a powerful message that the government is listening and is committed to providing quality services and high-performing programs. In the Punjab, citizens were grateful for the contact by the state. In a typical case, Noor Amin, who had property documents registered in Gujranwala district, wrote on April 11, 2014, in response to the government text message seeking his feedback, "Thanks for consulting me regarding your administration."

Communication to the wider public, to civil society, and to the media is important for the sake of transparency, citizen accountability, and compliance with increasingly stringent right to information legislation and its disclosure requirements. It is even more important to secure support and generate enthusiasm for what is going right. Consider the following true story of a missed opportunity to build on a tremendous success: The Balochistan Education Foundation (BEF) stands out in the vast, barren landscape of Pakistan's Balochistan province, the poorest province and a graveyard of failed education efforts. Among other duties, the foundation has the responsibility for funding remote rural communities that hire, pay, and monitor female teachers from among themselves. Between 2006 and 2009, the program had enrolled 27,888 children, including over 12,000 girls, at 649 schools (http://www.bef.org.pk/). It was an extraordinary achievement, but no one not directly involved in the foundation's efforts believed in the successful student enrollment rates. "It was just not possible; nothing would succeed here," said one skeptic (pers. comm.).

According to Zulfikar Hameed, the head of investigations and the force behind this effort, "The appeal of focusing limited resources on a small number of high-crime places is straightforward. If we can prevent crime at hot spot locations, then we might be able to reduce total crime," he said.

Communication to the wider public, to civil society, and to the media is important for the sake of transparency, citizen accountability, and compliance.

What if the project could be illustrated to skeptics with one photo after another?

Seeing is believing and date- and location-stamped photos are incontrovertible evidence.

In 2011, a meeting was held in Quetta, the provincial capital of Balochistan, with the province's governor and education department officials, who had long resented the autonomy of the BEF. Their cynicism pervaded the room. Several third-party studies had documented the good results, but no one present at the meeting was willing to accept that the reports were credible. What if the presentation of the education project could have been illustrated with one photo after another, on a giant screen, to skeptics in the government office? What if the BEF had flashed a series of vivid images of teachers and students, photographed daily since the project began? The evidence of success would have been overwhelming, and the critical funds and political leadership needed to sustain the foundation's work might have been more forthcoming. Seeing is believing, and date- and location-stamped photos are incontrovertible evidence that may even convince policy makers who do not believe that innovation can reclaim even the poorest areas.

Evidence must be presented so decision makers immediately "get it" Communication also must reach decision makers. Basex Research found that people switch activities every three minutes, including managers. The company looked at a number of activities of managers, including such things as reviewing documents (Feintuch, Goldes, and Spira 2005). Because of myriad distractions, communication with high-level officials must be credible, simple, action oriented, and in a format that highlights key messages immediately. Many attempts at evidence-based decision making fail because the evidence either is unconvincing or is not presented in a way that political and administrative leaders—who must contend with constraints on their time and attention—can use effectively. Therefore, a tool to process information and present it in ways that communicate with leaders effectively is essential. That tool is turning out to be the management dashboard.

Dashboards, or executive information systems, have been around for more than three decades. But they never became effective management tools, even in the private sector, because the underlying capacity to handle large amounts of data and present it to laypersons was not available (Few 2013).

A dashboard is similar to the cockpit of an airplane. The pilot is able to survey the status and performance of all relevant systems simultaneously, to know if they are operating correctly and whether adjustment of any element, such as altitude, speed, or course, is necessary. A dashboard measures and tracks programs or services to provide a snapshot at a particular point in time. It also tracks streams of data pertaining to a single data point to identify performance trends. Dashboards can provide very broad information or highly detailed information, to monitor such things as school attendance or the activities of health workers in the field on a daily or weekly basis.

A dashboard can also become an interactive communication space when it is integrated with SMS-based communication that relays information to managers and employees. The uptake of data entry from the field level improved substantially when the Punjab Information Technology Board (PITB) started sending monthly SMS messages back to the field officers with key pieces of information on their data entry performance. SMS-enabled discussion boards among field providers and managers can also nudge better use of the data. Discussion space for employees and managers, including SMS-based discussions and comments on performance, creates opportunity for problem solving, peer learning, and mutual comparison (the PITB is experimenting with such a space for health managers). This community of practice is possibly the most critical innovation in the dashboard's design and use of space and will help to improve performance.

Agriculture Extension: The Opportunity to Make Deeper Inroads

In Punjab, it is the job of the Provincial Agriculture Extension Directorate to deliver crop productivity information to farmers. Despite extensive institutional structures to provide timely and practical information, the directorate, like most government departments in developing countries, is inefficient.

The Punjab Agriculture Department, in collaboration with the Punjab Information Technology Board, piloted the use of smartphones in the districts of Faisalabad and Rajanpur to enhance existing monitoring systems and provide better information for decision making. The enhanced data collected included locations of extension staff, photos of their activities, the kind of activity performed, and a photo of the farmer they were working with. The main data fields include the farmer's name and mobile number, and the activity performed (farmer day, demonstration, supervision support, pest scouting, or monitoring of inputs such as fertilizer, pesticide, seed, and irrigation). The GPS location of the extension

Discussion space for employees and managers, including SMS-based discussions and comments on performance, creates opportunity for problem solving, peer learning, and mutual comparison (the PITB is experimenting with such a space for health managers).

agent, a photo of the activity, and a "selfie" (self-taken photo) of the officer are also included.

In the future the forms will be extended to capture data such as crop yields, pest details, and ultimately the entire field data reporting system. Accurate information on basic extension activities opens up new possibilities for creating evidence-based monitoring and incentive systems within the existing department structure.

Pictorial representation of data can be very powerful in its ability to provide basic but extremely valuable insights. For example, analysis of the spatial spread of agricultural extension staff, shown in figure 3.1, showed that extension activities were being carried out primarily along the major highway. The majority of farmers, who live in less-accessible villages, were likely not benefiting from any government extension activities. That information also raised the important question of how to create incentives for agriculture extension staff to get out into villages, to improve outreach and potentially improve farmer knowledge

Figure 3.1

Smartphone-Based Punjab Agricultural Activities Monitoring System in Rajanpur District

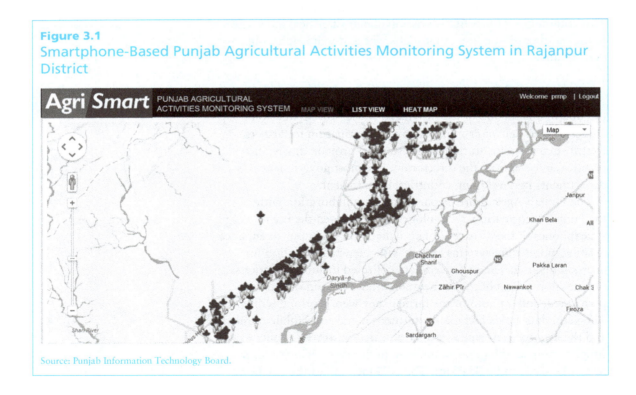

Source: Punjab Information Technology Board.

and practices. Moreover, data on extension activities also made possible an activity analysis indicating the various activities that the visits were devoted to and whether any particular activity was neglected or performed too often.

Communicating results (and even concerted efforts to seek results) back to the citizens will also help strengthen voice. When citizens learn through targeted or mass messages that their feedback is being used, as in the Punjab feedback effort, a virtuous cycle of more citizens reporting frankly about the services can start. Making the dashboards public will also help foster voice. With concrete feedback about service delivery to look at, media and civil society can also increase pressure on the government—again improved with the help of new social media channels—to improve service delivery. The Indian website, www.Ipaidabribe.com, among many such efforts in South Asia, aims to increase pressure on the government to improve services.

Solution 4. Nudging champions from above.
From our work helping countries design monitoring and evaluation systems around the world, we know that many leaders and government managers want a way to collect information about which programs are working and which ones are not. Despite the investments these countries make in building such systems, many are not used. Kusek, Gorgens, and Hamilton wrote in 2013 that these systems need strong enabling environments, including the backing of leaders and champions who are committed both to collecting trustworthy data and to using them for better decision making. As discussed in chapter 2, many of these systems don't offer information quickly enough for just-in-time problem solving. Champions and leaders move on, become involved in other problems, and the systems begin to languish. What we have found is needed is a clear message from on high that these systems are necessary and important, and this message must be sent throughout the organization.

Many of the smartphone reforms we reviewed were able to ensure the necessary "nudging" from above through the help of dashboards. Simple, clear information about the status of a field program, using summary dashboards, can provide busy senior officials with an immediate opportunity to intervene on problems and applaud successes. When information comes directly from the point of delivery and bypasses many routes of review, then it is possible that decisions can be made that address today's urgencies and not yesterday's unsolved problems.

Communicating results (and even concerted efforts to seek results) back to the citizens will also help strengthen voice.

Emperor Akbar and Secretary Mahmood knew nothing about electronic dashboards, but they did know something about the importance of voter approval and personal contact. This nudging sends a strong message to lower managers as well as average citizens that top leaders care about good government. For example, in Punjab, every citizen receives an automated call, recorded in the chief minister's voice, ahead of every text message, the content tailored to each service. The text message again is sent on behalf of the chief minister and addresses each citizen by his or her name, which is derived from the transaction information received in the system. When citizens reply, they are actually writing directly to the chief minister. (And because they know this, wedding invitations to the chief minister are not uncommon.) The value of this proactive communication to the chief minister is obvious. His voice and text messages reach out every single day to some 5,000 citizens who have actually received a service. Equally important is that once the chief minister has staked his political capital directly on the effort, he is also invested in doing something with the data (see box 3.3).

At their core, communication technologies are force-multiplying tools to reach leaders and other senior officials and encourage their commitment and involvement with reform. The chief minister of the Punjab province, for example, is a key champion of the proactive citizen feedback effort. However, he could not have extended his outreach to every corner of the province in a sustained, institutionalized manner without the cell phone architecture, the related telecom infrastructure, and the innovative, proactive outreach to citizens. Earlier methods of citizen outreach—courts or open forums where citizens would come to emperors and kings to lodge complaints—had not changed fundamentally for thousands of years. Now government officials have the means to reach hundreds of thousands of citizens with personalized messages and receive feedback about service delivery, even in developing countries.

Solution 5. Experimenting with several innovations simultaneously. Improving service delivery across large public systems is enormously difficult. Transplanting a successful institutional structure from one country to another often fails. Solutions therefore have to be very specific to the locality. Recognizing these well-known challenges, Pritchett (2013) has advocated for problem-driven efforts that

The value of this proactive communication to the chief minister is obvious. His voice and text messages reach out every single day to some 5,000 citizens who have actually received a service. Most politicians across the world would be interested in such numbers of citizen contacts.

Box 3.3
The Chief Minister's Call

Text of the automated call from the chief minister:

"Assalam O Alaikum. I, Muhammad Shahbaz Sharif, am speaking to you. Some time ago, you [had your property registered]. If you had to face any difficulties, or if someone received unfair gratification from you, or asked for such money; kindly do inform us. In relation to this, you will shortly receive a text from me from the number 8070. After reading this SMS, or having someone read it for you, please do reply."

Translated text of SMS message asking for feedback:

"Respected [Mr. name of citizen], you submitted a request for [service that was used] on [date]. Please let me know how your experience was—did you have to give a bribe? From, Shahbaz Sharif."

The specifics, shown in brackets, are mail-merged from the information sent from the field.

Examples of SMS responses from the live dashboard:

Tehsil Head Quarter Health unit - service accessed on 2014-03026:

Translated SMS response: "Staff provided us with good service. They did not take any money and prescribed medicine. We are now fine. Thank you Mr. Chief Minister Shahbaz Shareef. SHB."

Revenue Department- service accessed on 2014-03-18:

SMS response: "No they deal us very good we are very thanks to SHEGBAZ SHARIF."

Rescue 1122 - service accessed on 2014-04-14:

SMS response: "Dear Sir, Thanks for your message I called to 1122 for urgent emergency to drop my mom to Dr. Hospital the operator reply that the car is not available at the moment it will take time I again call after 10 minutes they again reply that the car will take time I said ok send but they did not arrived and my mom was in very critical condition; I took her in my car and dropped her in Shafi hospital emergency ward. From my first call the car arrived in 45 minutes in my home that is too much time and they went back. I request you to kindly upgrade the service system to arrive as early as possible when someone called on 1122 to save the life of human. Thank you very much. Muhammad Naeem"

Revenue Department- service accessed on 2014-03-12:

Translated SMS response: "Greetings! Sir we purchased a property worth 13,50000 which we paid a tax of PRs 100,000 and paid a bribe of PRs 50,000 for property registration."

Domicile- service accessed on 2014-04-05:

Translated SMS response: "No sir. Thanks to you for being busy serving your nation day and night."

encourage "positive deviance," focus on rapid learning, and diffuse lessons quickly among professional peers. Andrews, Pritchett, and Woolcock (2012) call this experimentation approach—as distinct from experiments—"problem-driven iterative adaptation." Although those experts are not explicit on methods, we have seen these principles at play in places where one might never expect reform to emerge, such as in Punjab, Pakistan, and Karnataka, India, and even Dhaka, Bangladesh, through experimenting, learning, and then mainstreaming.

Does this approach mean conducting large, expensive randomized experiments? Not necessarily. Such trials may be needed in certain cases. But what is needed more is expanding a project as necessary, with rapid feedback loops and iterative adaptation (Kusek, Gorgens, and Hamilton 2013). Dabholkar and Krishnan (2013) argue that although ideas are indeed important, the speed with which new ideas are brought to customers is far more important, for example, experimenting with low-cost projects at high speed, accelerating from demonstrating a prototype to incubation, and iterating quickly to improve on the business model. They cite the prolific inventor Thomas Edison, famous for his lightbulb and many lesser-known late-19th-century inventions, who worked on many ideas simultaneously in an "inventions factory" of sorts, using those innovation principles. Edison's strategy was to create a large pipeline and quickly roll out inventions. After testing each in the market or laboratory, he either abandoned or improved on them. Edison promised that he would deliver a minor invention every 10 days and a major invention every six months or so. He was true to his word, and throughout his lifetime faithfully delivered on that promise. "When I am after results that I have in mind," Edison said, "I may make hundreds or thousands of experiments out of which there may be one that promises results in the right direction. This I follow up to its legitimate conclusion, discarding the others, and usually get what I am after" (Ford and Crowther 2007).

As former public servants, we learned the importance of having the flexibility to experiment using different variables to achieve successful outcomes. The cost of learning, failing, and trying again with the new communication technologies is so low that experimentation is not as risky as it may seem. One champion at any management level, a few smartphones, an open source application, some basic running costs, a basic dashboard, and of

Edison's strategy was to create a large pipeline of experiments and quickly roll out inventions.

One champion at any management level, a few smartphones, an open source application, some basic running costs, a basic dashboard, and of course, a program to monitor, and you have the ingredients for reform.

course, a program to monitor, and you have the ingredients for reform. Providing space for experimentation is an essential and core part of our experience. Bottom-up learning can change frozen habits and structures and must be part of any larger effort to overhaul government delivery systems. Therefore, rule number 5 proposes that leaders and managers enable, allow, and push experimentation and facilitate the efforts of those in public sector systems who have the courage and drive to come with new ideas. We have found that efforts to change the way services are delivered have to build in experimentation, instead of starting from the blueprint. That is a major shift for officials and politicians who grew up in systems of due process and hierarchy, but some of the leaders mentioned in chapters 1 and 2 succeeded because they did just that.

The fundamental building blocks of the communication architecture, thanks to massive private sector innovation and investment, are already in place. Because access is often the biggest hurdle to development for the poorest in South Asia, increased connectivity will be the stepping-stone to greater inclusiveness, rapid innovation, increased voice, and many more opportunities. Governments have not really leveraged this architecture to transform the management of public services, but that is changing too. As was the case with other electronic media, such as television, the VCR, and the web, the cell phone was first used for personal family connections and entertainment and now is increasingly used for business, including government business.

Certainly some will refute and counter our argument with the one that places at greater importance to system-wide reforms. They might say that resolving government problems one at a time is unsustainable and is the wrong way to reform government. Nonetheless, in today's world, we do not have time to wait for reforms that might take years—not when tomorrow's leaders are playing games on smartphones by age three. With technology evolving so fast, other reforms based on knowledge not even imagined earlier will also likely be introduced.

A New Model for Experimenting and Reform

These solutions are not the only must-haves for successful mobile technology reforms to work. We believe, however, that since five have been present across all the successful reforms we reviewed, they should be included in the design of new mobile government innovations. We also emphasize that one size does not fit all. Local conditions may be the most important determinant of success, and all attempts to introduce reforms should be seen through that lens. We are excited about what is happening in South Asia, despite its current backdrop of opposition and challenge.

A Smart Proactive Government Model

We developed an innovation model called Smart Productive Government that integrates lessons learned across the five solutions. Building on the Proactive Feedback Scheme, the Smart Proactive Model shown in figure 3.2 is grounded in conventional results-based management, monitoring and evaluation principles, beneficiary feedback, and a use of GPS/GIS-enabled smartphones to monitor services being delivered directly at the point of delivery. With Smart Proactive Government, new reform practices can be introduced that replace paper-based data collection; emphasize proactive feedback collection instead of the standard, reactive, grievance-receiving mechanisms; push targeted performance analysis and results information to service

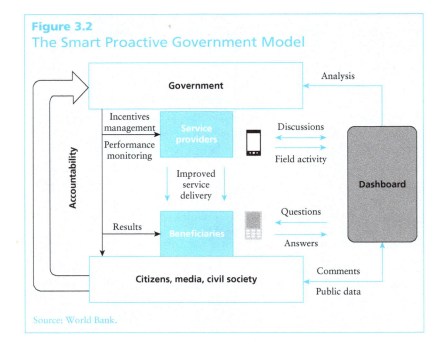

Figure 3.2
The Smart Proactive Government Model

Source: World Bank.

providers and identified beneficiaries; calibrate incentives and resources based on the improved quantity and quality of service delivery; promote discussions among service providers; and place digital data and information in the public domain for civil society and media oversight. Readers can find the nuts and bolts of how to implement this simple scheme at low cost in the appendix.

Conclusion—Still Many Barriers to Getting ICT Reforms Right

Despite almost universal excitement about mobile phone reforms, they are far from being sure things. Despite enthusiasm, significant new investments, and new leadership that is able to secure political backing for new schemes, dozens of these experiments have not worked out. Some of the failures stem from the most traditional of problems, such as failure to listen to beneficiaries, overdesigned expensive systems, poor sequencing of change management efforts, and a general resistance to change on the part of service providers and even beneficiaries. Although mobile phones are possibly the most accepted of all technologies, many governments have only begun to use them for the kind of core service improvements that this book argues for.

In many cases, the very fact that mobile and smart technologies are cheap is a reason for their rejection. In developing or emerging countries, information technology systems offer opportunities for large kickbacks. However, purchasing cheap Android phones, even in bulk, is not going to offer similar opportunities for graft, especially when every third citizen on the street knows their price. Another risk to the success of these technologies is resistance to a system that aggressively monitors service provider performance. Sanitation workers in Lahore have regularly demonstrated against photo-enforced monitoring by the Lahore Waste Management Company (*The News* 2014). Although photo and location data, and even their specificity and timeliness, will help to check dishonesty, gaming the system is not impossible. In Punjab, Pakistan, field officials have resorted to entering invalid cell numbers or the cell numbers of middlemen to attempt to subvert the government effort to seek feedback. Attention paid to data quality is key to the success of these efforts. In the Punjab Citizen Feedback Project, for example, before a district is held accountable for its stated performance on citizen feedback, the data collected are audited for quality.

Mobile phones also have not completely bridged the gender or the poverty divide. In South Asia, the level of gender disparity in education varies. In most countries female literacy is low, as are women's participation in the labor force and their representation in public administration and politics. The Cherie Blair Foundation for Women (2010) and others have explored how mobile technology could help alleviate or remove some of the constraints that prevent women and girls from being part of the digital world. Some of the barriers are those that prevent women's empowerment and gender equality, such as illiteracy, lack of skills and information and the high costs of acquiring them, and culture and religious traditions. The biggest gender barrier may be the human and cultural context. For example, group or self-photos of female workers may not be possible in many Pakistan settings.

This gap can be bridged, but exclusive reliance on new technologies may not completely address the problem. In the Punjab proactive feedback collection efforts and literacy and access barriers are being tackled by employing call agents who, based on the district of the citizen, employ the local dialect to converse. Mobilizing female workers in difficult security environments may be a challenge, but hiring female call agents to speak to the females of the household, without any attendant cultural or security issue, is not. In the Punjab ICT-based School Council Mobilization Program, after reports from the field that males were not happy that women school council members were being called by male agents, the program established a procedure that only females may call female school council members. Similarly, only female agents call to ask about the quality of female indoor health care in the feedback model.

Another barrier is the resigned acceptance of, or even collusion with, petty corruption in many countries in South Asia. As seen in the Punjab Citizen Feedback example, it can complicate efforts to obtain proactive feedback. When contacted by call agents many citizens acknowledged that they paid bribes but said they did not mind. Paying a hefty tip after concluding a land transaction was customary, and money changed hands in the spirit of celebration. Other citizens may be jumping the queue or may be colluding with field officials to rob the state. In those cases, proactive collection of feedback, even by a highly responsible senior official, will not help. Also, increased trustworthiness of data and shorter collection and reporting times will not override poor program design and planning. If government does not have a "clear idea of the goals and objectives of a particular data collection effort, it won't matter what technology is chosen to make it happen" (Trucano 2014). An early effort to introduce use of smartphones in the teacher training wing of the Punjab education department failed because senior officials could not agree on what data to collect.

We think that perhaps the greatest challenge is a traditional one. That is, regardless of the technology used, reform will not be successful if government leaders and ordinary civil servants are not held accountable to do their jobs. Mobile technology can indeed improve channels of communication, from the citizen to the policy makers and from the policy makers to service providers, but policy makers still feel little pressure and exert feeble management. Put another way, improving the quality and timeliness of data collection is necessary, but is it sufficient to improve service delivery? How will the feedback loop be closed, so that data are used for corrective actions? Careful crafting of incentives along the chain of service delivery is equally necessary to sustain the impact of increased internal transparency beyond the initial scarecrow effect. "It is incentives that matter if politicians and service providers are to act on information and data," according to Foresti (2014).

A detailed discussion of what incentives will work in particular situations is beyond the scope of this book, but we suggest some solutions to meet this complicated challenge. The solution of "nudging champions" provides some ideas on how to motivate and empower leaders to communicate directly with citizens and act to redress systemic problems. The solution of communicating with common dashboards suggests other ideas. Making specific performance data or actual citizen feedback public—only the passwords of closed government sites need to be removed—will also foster media and civil society engagement and create pressure for policy makers to take action. Collection, analysis, and circulation of high-quality performance information can also help push middle managers and service providers to improve their act. In Punjab, where the authors met with workers grumbling about the new

Collection, analysis, and circulation of high-quality performance information can also help push middle managers and service providers to improve their act.

As long as beneficiaries can be identified on the basis of some characteristics of their telecom use— location based on the local cell phone tower, for example—feedback can be sought from them about any local service.

monitoring tools, they also met officials happily recording their activities with smartphones. Development of low-tech, SMS-based, interactive discussion and comments space on the management dashboard, as is being attempted in Punjab, will foster both peer learning and competition. If financial incentives are needed in any particular situation, the increasingly ubiquitous mobile payment solutions allow inventive, periodic solutions with low transaction costs and extreme accuracy.

On balance, we have described here just initial efforts, scratching the surface of the possibilities to improve government accountability, transparency, and citizen voice and the capacity of the politicians to hear it. Going forward, the potential is limitless. Proactive government is possible. As long as beneficiaries can be identified on the basis of some characteristics of their telecom use—location based on the local cell phone tower, for example— feedback can be sought from them about any local service. Moreover, more and more governments are realizing that despite the lack of trustworthy data, they can still get immediate feedback on how well (or not) programs are working in even the most remote areas of their countries.

We recognize there are challenges. Yet we argue that basic ideas of improved data collection, proactive citizen engagement, evidence-based decision making, transparency, and communication can help drive change in any context. Our solutions are not costly to implement in time or money.

To some readers, the stories we have told in this book might sound unrealistic and unsustainable because of the countries and the region in which they have been introduced. Not so. With a proposed $20 smartphone the continued rapid penetration of the Internet these technologies are becoming commonplace. We argue for leveraging the present and the future possibilities of the new communication infrastructure. Like everything else, the public sector will have to change. With active adoption of these solutions, we think it will change faster.

References

Andrews, M., L. Pritchett, and M. Woolcock. 2012. *Escaping Capability Traps through Problem-Driven Iterative Adaptation (PDIA)*. Center for Global Development Working Paper 299, Washington, DC.

Banerjee, A., R. Banerji, E. Duflo, R. Glennerster, and S. Khemamni. 2010. "Pitfalls of Participatory Programs: Evidence from a Randomized Evaluation in Education in India." *American Economic Journal - Economic Policy* 2 (1): 1–30.

Cherie Blair Foundation for Women, GSMA Development Fund, and Vital Wave Consulting. 2010. "Women and Mobile: A Global Opportunity. A Study on the Mobile Phone Gender Gap in Low and Middle-Income Countries." Cherie Blair Foundation for Women, London.

Dabholkar, V., and R. Krishnan. 2013. "Evolution of Innovative Processes: From Edison to Lafley." Catalign Innovation Consulting. http://www .catalign.com.

Duflo, E., P. Dupas, and M. Kremer. 2007. "Peer Effects, Pupil-Teacher Ratios, and Teacher Incentives in Kenya." Poverty Action Lab, Boston.

Feintuch, J., D. Goldes, and G. Spira. 2005. "The Cost of Not Paying Attention: How Interruptions Impact Knowledge Worker Productivity." Basex Consulting, Inc., New York.

Few, Stephen, 2013. *Information Dashboard Design: Displaying Data for At-A-Glance Monitoring.* 2d ed. Oakland, CA. Analytics Press.

Ford, H., and S. Crowther. 2007. *Edison As I Know Him.* Whitefish, MT: Kessinger Publishing.

Foresti, Marta. 2014. "An Overview: The 'Then and Now' of Public Service Delivery." Public Service at the Cross Roads, WDR anniversary conference, February 28–March 1, World Bank, Washington, DC.

Jha, A. K. 2006. "Use of Geo-informatics in Granting Forest Rights Act in the State of Maharashtra." Tribal Research and Training Institute presentation.

Kusek, J., M. Gorgens, and B. Hamilton. 2013. *Fail-Safe Management: Five Rules to Avoid Project Failure.* Washington, DC: World Bank.

Madon, Shirin. 2014. "Information Tools for Improving Accountability in Primary Health Care: Learning from the Case of Karnataka." In *Closing the Feedback Loop: Can Technology Bridge the Accountability Gap,* edited by Bjorn-Soren Gigler and Savita Bailur, 189–209. Washington, DC: World Bank.

The News. 2014. "Rift between LWMC, Sanitary Workers Deepens," May 13. Accessed July 18 at http://www.thenews.com.pk/ Todays-News-5-250319-Rift-between-LWMC,-sanitary-workers-deepens.

Rahman, N., et al. 2011. *Ecosystem for the Mahatma Gandhi National Rural Employment Guarantee Scheme. ICT Facilitated Access to Information Innovations: A Compendium of Case Studies from South Asia.* WBI and OneWorld Research.

Rosenberg, Tina. 2012. "Armed with Data, Fighting More than Crime." *New York Times,* May 2.

Saif, Umar. 2014. "Using Technology to Help Citizens." *Express Tribune*, May 23.

Trucano, M. 2014. "EduTech: A World Bank Blog on ICT Use in Education" (blog), April 25. http://blogs.worldbank.org/edutech /using-mobile-phones-data-collection-some-questions-consider.

World Bank. 2014. *Third Party Monitoring Program for the Afghanistan Reconstruction Trust Fund: A Review.* Washington, DC: World Bank.

Looking under the Hood of the Smart Proactive Government Model

This appendix is intended as a handbook and guide for any organization considering introducing or experimenting with Smart Proactive Government. From our personal experience, especially introducing smart management in Pakistan, we want to share what we have learned—about what works and what we know might cause the effort to fail. Our model, shown in figure A.1, solves some of the issues of what has been called "the long route of accountability" for service delivery (World Bank, *World Development Report 2004*). It creates a shorter route, whereby citizens can hold service providers to account directly. The Smart Proactive Government model makes use of ICT technology to achieve that goal, replacing paper-based data collection with smartphones. It emphasizes proactive feedback collection, instead of the standard, reactive grievance-receiving mechanisms, pushing performance analysis and results information to both service providers and identified beneficiaries. It promotes discussions among service providers and making digital data and information public for civil society and media oversight. The scheme relies on several loops of communication between beneficiaries and service providers, to ensure that information moves rapidly from citizen-client directly to decision makers.

Smart Proactive Government Uses Four Tools

The Smart Proactive Government model may not be right for all governments and all services. In some situations and for some services, traditional, paper-based systems may continue to make the most sense. Every organization and government must decide what makes the most sense for them based on factors such as cost and capacity. Smart proactive government uses four information and communication technology (ICT) tools: short messaging

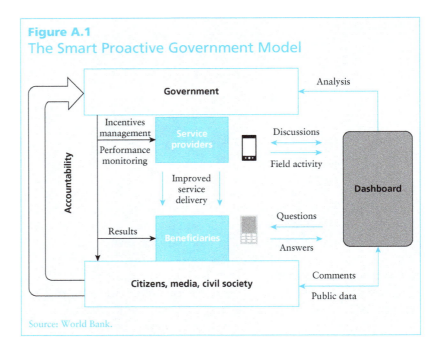

Figure A.1
The Smart Proactive Government Model

Source: World Bank.

service (SMS), call centers, smartphones, and dashboards. We also present a number of ways to use them as a modern monitoring and evaluation tool, to help governments ensure that their decisions are based on evidence.

As discussed in this book, the ability of these ICT tools to collect information at minimal cost—including new kinds of information, such as geo-tagged locations, in-field photos, and beneficiary feedback—enables managers in a vast variety of situations to make informed decisions with better and more timely data, visual and spatial evidence, and beneficiary feedback.

Choose the Right Technology for Smart Proactive Government

The choice of a smart management instrument largely depends on the problem to be addressed, the scope of the activity, the literacy levels of the target population, and the cost constraints, among other factors. The following is a list of factors that should inform the choice:

- *Scope of the activity*. For a very small data collection activity with good quality supervision, even a paper-based system could be sufficient. For larger undertakings, solutions based on information and communication technology (ICT) should be adopted, and depending on their scope, different variants of ICT tools need to be explored.

- *Capital and recurrent costs.* While the onetime cost of setting up the system and training people to use it is the primary concern, the recurrent costs of licenses, connectivity, electricity, maintenance, and manpower, although they are low and falling, also need to be carefully considered.

- *Nature of the data collection activity.* A primary determinant of the instrument selected is the kind of data to be collected. For example, it may be monitoring data from the public field staff, open-ended feedback from a particular audience, or geo-tagged pictures documenting in-field activities. The information that needs to be gathered will determine which instrument works best.

- *Electricity issues.* The presence or stability of the electricity supply or a battery charging facility is another factor that could influence the choice of tool, as system breakdowns could hamper the overall efficiency of the data collection exercise.

- *Telecom connectivity.* Because the timeliness of data is one of the biggest advantages of ICT-based methods, it is important to compare different instruments' telecom connectivity. Data can still be collected offline, but their timeliness and security could diminish if due care is not taken.

- *Audience.* The target population may be government agents or the general public, whose literacy levels and technical knowledge about ICT tools will be a concern.

Short Message Service, or SMS

All mobile phones are equipped with the capability to both send and receive text messages, more commonly known in some parts of the world as SMS, or short message service. It is one of the simplest mobile interactions. Text exchanged over SMS is electronic data. SMS can be used for short surveys or questionnaires, voluntary reporting, assessments, and even longitudinal studies. SMS-based methods can be used to collect data in two different ways:

String-based data entry requires the user to enter data by sending an SMS message in a predefined format, with different fields separated by a special character. The software translates information into different data fields. For example, consider a situation in which a designated official, such as a nurse in a remote health facility, wishes to report the name, phone number, and type of service for a patient served. Figure A.2 depicts how this information could be reported via a string-based SMS data entry. The method works well for internal staff, as they can quite easily be trained to follow the defined format. It becomes cumbersome, however, when the number of variable fields is large or, for example, if all the fields are numeric and their order is mistakenly changed, something the software cannot detect.

Question and answer–based data entry is a method that makes it feasible to enter more or more complex data and that is useful when users cannot be rigorously trained. Instead of the user

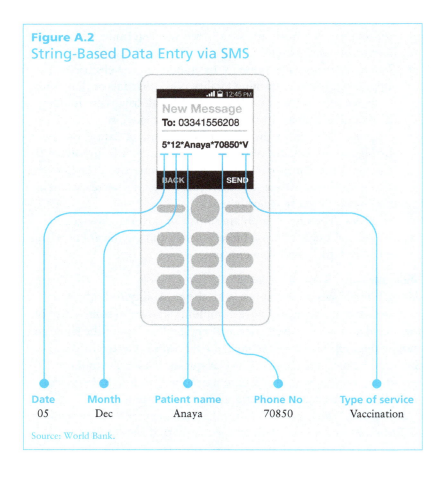

Figure A.2
String-Based Data Entry via SMS

Date	Month	Patient name	Phone No	Type of service
05	Dec	Anaya	70850	Vaccination

Source: World Bank.

composing and sending data in a predefined string format, the system triggers questions, one at a time, for the user to answer. Each answer can be verified for format and other basic logic to improve the data quality. Questions can be preprogrammed to change depending on the answer. Relatively complex surveys can also be easily conducted with this methodology. If the answer to a question is qualitative, every answer will have to be categorized by back end workers based on agreed protocols, as is done in the Punjab Feedback Model. With carefully designed quality checks, the subjective categorization could also be crowd-sourced. For example, an SMS feedback message would be categorized as a report of corruption only when three or more independent readers so describe it.

Benefits of SMS-Based Tools

- **They are extremely cheap and portable.** Mobile phones are extremely low cost, portable, and owned by almost everyone. The cost of SMS, depending on the package, could also be low or even negligible.
- **They have good connectivity options.** Mobile connectivity is almost ubiquitous and available at a negligible monthly cost.
- **No technical skill is required.** Given the pervasiveness of mobile phones, almost everyone can operate them with little or no assistance. Consequently there is no need to hire additional skilled technical staff or provide extensive training.
- **Data validation checks.** Data validation checks can be built into the server side of the data collection system. Error messages to the user can be generated automatically in case of an erroneous data entry. That reduces noise in the data set.
- **Real-time data availability.** Data collected from the field can be submitted immediately, eliminating the need for data entry operators and compilation delays. Data become visible in an online dashboard almost as they are submitted.
- **Customizability and ease of development.** Because the SMS tool relies on the exchange of messages to collect data, SMS-based data collection methods can be customized for different situations very easily. For example, they can be used for onetime feedback, for multiple question surveys, or for simple information dissemination in the form of alerts.

- **They can be merged with a database.** Messages can be merged with a database of beneficiary names and other data features to create a more personalized message, including use of different choices of language.
- **Data analysis is made easy.** Because the data received at the central server are validated and formatted, reports of various kinds can be generated automatically. The data can also be made readily available in usable formats for custom analyses.
- **Location can be tracked using SIMs.** The SIM, or subscriber identity module, is the chip placed inside every mobile phone to identify the subscriber. The SIM can help to pinpoint the location of the phone's user at a given time. SIMs are not as accurate as the smartphone's GPS facility, but if an accuracy of 2 or 3 km is sufficient, assuming tightly located towers, then SIMs can also serve the purpose of ensuring that the person using the phone to submit data did in fact visit the site.

Because nearly all users have at least a feature phone and are familiar with SMS, training for SMS-based data collection activities can focus more on building familiarity with required reporting formats. The tricky part of SMS data entry, especially string-based, is entering data in the correct format. Tools can be provided to make it easier to send an SMS in the right format, such as a preprinted table on paper, with fields in the correct order. The Punjab Information Technology Board (PITB) has developed an "SMS wheel." This is a system that makes it possible to send complex data in a simple manner from any feature phone to a central server. Figure A.3 shows a photo of the PITB disease surveillance SMS wheel. When the chosen information—number of cases, disease to report, day of the month—is lined up under the boxes on the left side, a string of numbers appears on the right side. The person reporting the data (from remote rural units, in this case) only has to send an SMS with this string of numbers to a designated number, and the needed information (disease reports, in this case) will be captured.

Limitations

- **Identification of the sender.** The location of a mobile phone can be tracked within a few kilometers, but without a photo or

Figure A.3
Punjab's SMS Wheel for Disease Surveillance Reporting

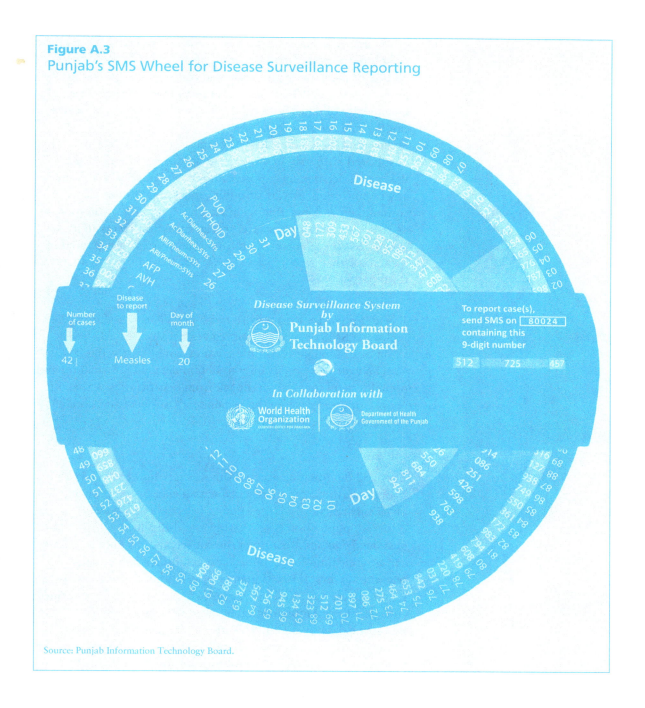

Source: Punjab Information Technology Board.

other biometric information it is impossible to verify whether the person purportedly sending data is also present at the location.

- **Nature of the data.** Digitization and transmission of data are improved, but data credibility cannot be checked with SMS.
- **Complexity of data.** With more data, mobile phone data entry can become cumbersome.
- **Privacy and legal issues.** In many regions (as in Pakistan), sending unsolicited SMS may be considered illegal. For example, the Pakistan Telecommunication Authority's regulation states that any organization, private or public, must obtain individuals' consent before contacting them via phone or SMS. Moreover, as an added security measure, special care must be taken to ensure that the telephone numbers of individuals are secured in a database that is encrypted and are not shared freely with any third party.

Call Centers to Support Proactive Feedback

A call center provides for a way to reach people who are not skilled enough to use SMS or who cannot read texts. Voice or call-based collection or dissemination of information can be costly, but it provides an excellent opportunity to obtain detailed information and is especially useful to collect feedback from beneficiaries. Each call is an opportunity to explore the respondent's answers and obtain multidimensional feedback (see figure A.4).

Benefits of Hiring a Call Center

- **Easy and far-reaching access.** Almost every household has a phone today and can be reached with a call. In comparison, physically reaching a large number of people or a widely dispersed population is very costly and difficult.
- **Sustained contact.** Because of the convenience of phones, calling can be a medium for sustained contact, unlike individual, onetime surveys. It opens many possibilities for continuous, long-term contact. Call-based methods can be used for sustained engagement and mobilization efforts over time.
- **Real-time data availability.** With an efficient third-party call center managing call volume and collecting responses, data are immediately uploaded in an online dashboard. Information can be categorized and analyses generated automatically. Such rapid availability also makes calls ideal for complaint management.

Figure A.4
The Citizen Feedback Model Call Center—How It Works

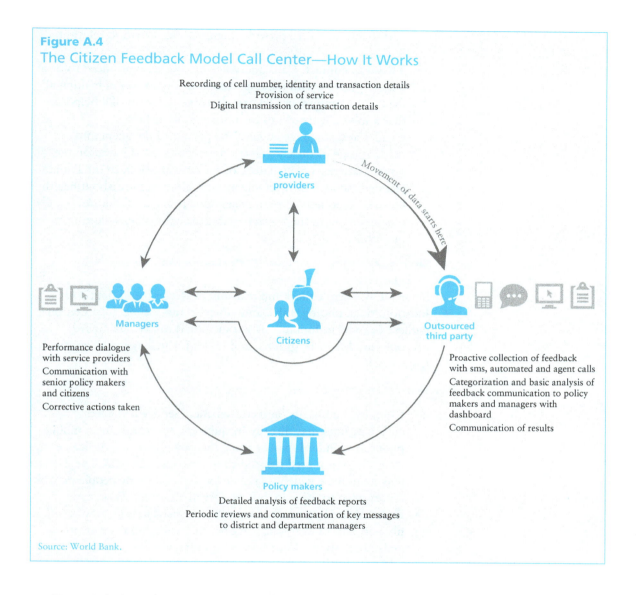

Source: World Bank.

- **Data analysis made easy.** Because the data received at the central server are validated and formatted, reports of various kinds can be generated automatically. Information can be visualized in the form of maps, tables, graphs, time trends, comparisons, and so forth.
- **Automatic information dissemination.** So-called robocalls, which are recorded audio messages delivered to mobile phones, can be recorded beforehand and automatically sent to particular people

at different times, to provide them with information relevant to them.

- **Two-way contact.** Calls and voice messages do not need to be a one-way street, with the department or organization making all the calls. Communication can also take the form of a help line that allows clients to call for information or help.
- **Gender and language choice.** The gender of the agent and the language of the conversation can be selected based on the target audience or the nature of the conversation. In the Punjab feedback model, only female agents call to inquire about health services, especially maternity services, because of cultural sensitivity about men—even male family members—asking such questions.

Smartphones for Immediate Performance Monitoring, Transparency, and Accountability

Smartphones help collect and transmit evidence-based data with location, time, photographs, and video or audio clips. Information gathered can be instantaneously transmitted to live dashboards with preconfigured reports, graphs, and tables for management review (figure A.5).

Benefits of Using Smartphones to Collect Data

- **Ubiquity, familiarity, and convenience.** Service providers collecting data may already be quite comfortable using a mobile phone (and indeed may be using their own personal device), even if they have not used it specifically for collecting data. The devices may already be widely available locally, and many people may be accustomed to using mobile phones in a variety of contexts.
- **Reduced training needs.** Given the pervasiveness of mobile phones, almost everyone can operate them with little or no assistance, and so less technical training may be necessary. In addition, with smartphones, and to a lesser extent with feature phones, help files and on-screen prompts can provide useful support and guidance that reinforces messages from any training that occurs and may obviate the need for some sorts of training altogether.
- **Low power.** Compared with devices such as laptops, mobile phones may be much easier to keep charged, as they require much less power. Many fast, low-cost charging options may be available in local communities because people are already

Figure A.5

Conversion of Paper Forms into Smartphone-Based Forms Using Open Data Kit

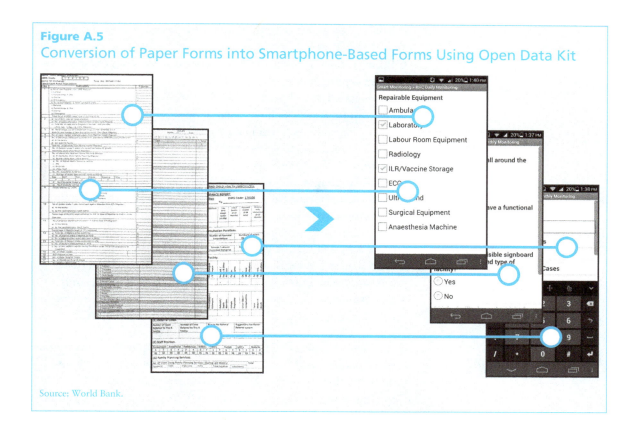

Source: World Bank.

using them for other purposes as part of their daily lives (Trucano 2013).

- **Data validation checks.** Data validation checks can be built into the application that is used to collect data. That augments data quality by discouraging entry of data that are either invalid or incorrect. For example, checks can prevent entry of letters in the blank for a phone number or ensure that the date of death of a patient can never be before the date of birth.
- **Capture of different types of data.** In addition to text, smartphones can also collect photos, audio, and video, read barcodes, and indicate GPS locations. If a building being surveyed is described as "damaged," for example, a picture can provide documentation. In addition, GPS or geo-location data can be collected and transmitted along with survey data. That information can be used in mapping the location of hospitals or

schools or to prove that an enumerator actually visited a place that they claimed to have visited.

- **Offline storage.** In areas with low connectivity data can be entered on the device and saved offline.
- **Customizability and ease of use.** Several open-source data collection frameworks have been developed for Android phones and tablets, such as Open Data Kit (ODK; www.opendatakit.org). The open-source frameworks make data collection using the Android phone very easy. The application can be customized to local languages and allows the use of pictorial interfaces and icons instead of text for low-literacy users. For example, the Information Technology University in Lahore, working with the PITB, is building a plug-and-play platform for data collection that is designed for the government's local requirements. Some of its features are localized language, an icon-based interface for low-literacy users, better management of field force, and so forth. An icon-based application used by the Punjab government to track the spread of dengue fever is shown in figure A.6.

Which Device to Choose? The basic functions required are available in all smartphones, but Android phones in particular have some additional benefits. Android is an open-source platform for mobiles, and compared to other platforms, many low-cost options are available, including open-source data collection applications. Moreover, reasonably priced local brands have gained a large share of the market. Among the options available are smartphones, tablets, and lately, "phablets," or large-screen phones. Among the considerations in smartphone selection are the following:

- *Cost* of the smartphone.
- *Warranty* as part of the purchase.
- *Screen display size*. Screen size may be relevant depending on the kind of activity. For example, a simple data collection effort might be easily carried out on a 3-inch screen. But a mobile-based community training initiative in the field might be more effective on a bigger screen.
- *The phone's power and memory capacity*. A finalized mobile phone survey is to be stored in the phone's memory. The volume of data collected and how often the material is synchronized (synced) or transferred onto the server should determine the size of the internal memory that the phones should have.

Figure A.6

Icon-Based Application from the Punjab Information Technology Board for Tracking Dengue Fever

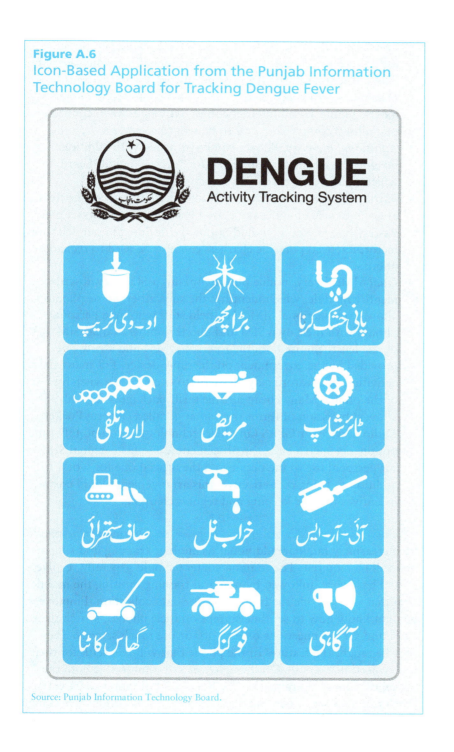

Source: Punjab Information Technology Board.

- *The Global Positioning System, or GPS.* Because geo-tagged locations and pictures are generally included in any field-based data collection effort, GPS is often a necessary phone feature.
- *Data Transfer Connectivity.* The phones should have either mobile phone–based Internet connectivity or a Wi-Fi connection that allows completed forms to be sent to a server.
- *Additional memory.* Phones can be provided with additional memory by means of a small SD (for "secure digital") card, onto which finalized forms can be saved.
- *Battery life.* Because electricity is a concern in most of the field areas, procuring phones with good battery life is always a plus. Battery life, however, should not be the deciding phone selection factor. External portable chargers can also be used to recharge phones.
- *Dual SIMs.* Every mobile phone contains a SIM, or subscriber identity module, which identifies the subscriber. Some phones allow two functional SIMs. For field staff who own personal phones with their own SIM and phone number, a dual-SIM phone lets them use both their personal SIM and a new one provided by the government on the same device. For many field activities, this feature may be useful to encourage ownership of the phone. Many cheap airtime tariff packages may only allow submission of forms over what is called General Pocket Radio Service, or GPRS (an older technology), with no talk time options. In such a case, the official could use his personal SIM for personal use of the phone and the official one for work. In addition to being cost-effective, this arrangement would create incentives for safe keeping and regular charging.

Training Needed for Smart Phone Monitoring Although smartphones are increasingly familiar, additional technology training and support may still be required. The training content should generally revolve around hardware, followed by practical training in using the mobile form that will provide the framework for data collection. Employees may not know how to set time stamps on their phones, switch their Wi-Fi and GPS connections on and off, or use touch screens. They must be taught the features of the phone that will be useful for their data collection exercise. Once employees are comfortable with the device, they must be trained on the basic rules of mobile data entry. That includes a set of best practices, such as always double checking time stamps, switching off GPS after recording a certain location to save battery life, paying attention to typical data entry errors while using touch screens, and watching for missing information. They must make sure they understand the form, including which questions to skip and which must be completed. Once the basics of data entry are covered, training should include reviewing the mobile application form in detail. That includes explaining each question on the form; defining the different fields; and demonstrating how to enter data on the phone, how to proceed from one question to another by swiping back and forth through the form, and how to send data electronically. Training videos could be created and installed on the phones, with a quick overview of data entry and common problems and solutions. Mobile-based quizzes or tests can also be conducted after training to ensure that the participants absorbed the material and to assess the quality of the training.

Limitations and Challenges

- **Cost.** Though falling every day, cost is still a consideration, and it should be seen in the context of the likely benefits. As of now GPS/GIS–enabled smartphones are still too costly for many people living in developing countries, and their distribution may be limited. This can limit the scope of the monitoring effort that is undertaken.
- **Discomfort due to changes in the status quo.** One challenge that many groups face, especially government agencies that implement large-scale data collection, is resistance to innovation and change. Increased efficiency resulting from mobile data collection efforts may be seen as threatening the livelihoods of individual workers and the viability of existing institutional structures.
- **Privacy and legal issues.** Tracking people's movements and collecting data without their informed consent may be illegal. In fact, as of June 25, 2014, the Supreme Court of the United States recognized the vast amount of personal information contained in a mobile phone and ruled that police need a warrant to search the mobile phones of people they arrest. In the case of government program monitoring, legal constraints may not apply. Because the device being used typically belongs to the government or organization and is issued to the employees, any data obtained through the device are, according to most legal interpretations, the issuing authority's property.
- **Data security and privacy.** Digital collection and transmission of data, as parts of a large data collection effort, have potential

risks related to security and privacy that are often fundamentally different from those associated with traditional paper surveys. Data stored on devices or being transmitted can be stolen or improperly accessed. Because of the potential to link individual data points with both geographic location (as a result of GPS) and individual people (data may, for example, be attributed to specific phones at specific times of day), the privacy implications may well warrant special attention.

In addition, the sponsoring organization would do well to ensure that it retains (for example) usage rights (if not full ownership) to the data collected and to consider, at each stage of the data collection and sharing process, who holds the rights to the data collected and what they are permitted (and not permitted) to do with it. The use of encryption, both at the device level and during transmission, can greatly mitigate the risks. But the operation of digital data security tools, protocols, and good practices, as well as related regulatory frameworks, laws, and guidelines governing their use, may not be widely known, and in some places may not even have been developed.

Where third-party vendors or tools are used during the mobile data collection process—as is usually the case—care needs to be taken to ensure that the ownership, possession, and use of data collected and transmitted are clearly articulated. Sufficient mechanisms need to be in place to audit the related arrangements and agreements and to ensure that penalties for noncompliance are clear and enforceable (Trucano 2013).

- **Ensuring data quality.** Using appropriate software on the devices can easily prevent scamming of location, photos, or time stamps. Some security features that the software should have, but which are currently absent from open-source platforms, include the following:

  A feature to prevent faking photos by attaching old photographs instead of taking them on location. This feature would force the camera to take a picture at the time of the message.

  A feature to prevent changing the time setting of the device. It should fetch a time stamp from a trusted online server, if an Internet connection is available, or from the GPS satellite.

A feature to prevent someone from bypassing the device's built-in GPS device. It should fetch the location directly from the GPS.

A function to control the time between the taking of a photo and recording the location. The interval should be restricted to a few minutes or less, depending on the application's need. If the time exceeds the predefined limit, both the picture and the location must be taken again.

Encryption of data. Data encryption ensure that data are garbled and cannot be manually edited once entered; it is equivalent to bypassing the data entry application. If it were possible to edit the data manually while the information is stored on the phone, before submission, any checks and data validation in the app would be void.

Common Maintenance Challenges and Solutions

Theft. To counter theft, policy should be that if a device is stolen, damaged, or misplaced, the employee is responsible to replace it. This is standard policy in Punjab and has worked smoothly, with little resistance and almost no reports of damaged or lost phones.

Charging. In places with power shortages, and where service is frequently interrupted, phone users spending extensive time in the field may have difficulty keeping their phones charged on a daily basis. Solar chargers are a cheap and portable solution that can be used anywhere. They can be used directly or together with an uninterruptible power source, or UPS, to charge the battery. Vehicle chargers or other kinds that turn movement—for example, the rotation of a motorcycle's wheels—into electricity may also be explored.

Some Related Questions about Data Collection Using Smartphones

Even where there is agreement on the potential usefulness of deploying mobile phones as part of a data collection effort, certain questions are important to consider and plan out during the initial stages.

- *What are the main goals of the data collection effort being considered?* If a sponsoring group does not have a clear idea of the goals and objectives of its project, then it won't matter what technology is chosen to carry it forward. There is a saying to the effect that if you are pointed at the wrong target, introducing a new technology can help get you there faster. Opportunities to collect data quickly and cheaply using innovative processes can be enticing, but it is important to remember that whatever technologies are chosen are just means to an end, not ends in themselves.

- *To what extent can mobile data collection efforts be handled in-house, and to what extent will they need to be outsourced to others?* Initial mobile data collection efforts may often be planned and implemented by groups outside existing data collection processes. The reasons for this can be quite understandable. The ability to use new mobile technologies for such purposes may be considered (rightly or wrongly) outside the competence of many traditional actors. That is especially the case when such efforts are in their early or pilot stages. As the efforts become more widespread, costly, and strategic, however, care should be taken to ensure that, at a minimum, sufficient competency exists within the sponsoring organization to allow staff to plan and direct operations and evaluate their efficacy, even if mobile data collection activities are largely implemented by third parties.

- *Is there sufficient local capacity to plan, implement, and sustain mobile data collection efforts?* Whoever is responsible for mobile data collection efforts in their initial stages, it may be important over time that the operations are increasingly led and implemented by local groups, whether from the public or private sector, civil society, or academia. Indeed, the project's sustainability over time may well depend on the development of supporting ecosystems of local actors and expertise.

- *How will new systems to collect data using mobile devices integrate with existing information systems and processes?* Care should be taken to ensure that the results of mobile data collection efforts can be absorbed into existing information management systems. If the systems are incompatible, the operation of essentially parallel systems may be expedient in the short run but will be costly and inefficient over the long term. The introduction of mobile data collection may expose deficiencies in existing information systems and be a catalyst for upgrading legacy systems. Integrating the tools and processes of mobile data collection, as well as the data that it generates, is best considered as part of an overall planning process for the collection, sharing, analysis, and storage of related data.

- *Who are the key stakeholders and partners who will need to be engaged during the mobile data collection effort, and what are the key components of their engagement?*
- *What is the likelihood that stakeholders will buy into the plan has to be evaluated.* There must be an understanding with both government managers and service providers concerning how the collected data will integrate into, or operate separately from, their existing information systems. Efforts to collect data through the use of mobile phones may require that new partnerships be established, some of them with nontraditional partners. At the same time, the nature of partnerships and interactions with existing stakeholder groups may change as well. Sponsoring groups would do well to map out the universe of key stakeholder groups, attempt to analyze and predict the impact of mobile data collection efforts on them, and plan accordingly.

Moving from paper-based to ICT-based data collection has created countless new opportunities in managing government. Some have been tested and are available, and other applications are still incubating. Real-time data collection that includes locations and photos can revolutionize monitoring. It could be used not only for daily monitoring but also to facilitate higher-level decisions, such as calculating incentives, field allowances, and resource allocations.

A few of the many possible applications of SMS, call centers, and smartphones are described below.

Using SMS for Budget Tracking

The process of collecting simple numbers can become difficult and complicated when the information needs to be collected from many different places and people. For example, tracking budgets for small government entities is one example of a difficult task that can be easily resolved through SMS-based data reporting.

For example, keeping track of the budget for the school council— the official title of the parent teacher committee—of each government school in Punjab (some 60,000 of them) has always been a challenge. To address it, the Punjab government is experimenting with a simple SMS-based data collection method whereby specific members of each council are asked for their budget once every month. They are sent simple questions, one after another, to collect the necessary information. The questions include, for example, How much money was allocated to the school council? How much was spent on furniture this month? How much was spent on infrastructure? and so on. All the responses to these questions are then automatically collected in an Excel spreadsheet that can be analyzed. This mechanism can be taken a step further by sending the councils monthly alerts informing them how much money is left in their accounts.

Day-to-Day Data Collection

Punjab government's Lady Health Worker program is an example of a vastly spread out program. With 47,000 Lady Health Workers (LHWs) attached to the department of health, it is impossible for the department to equip all of them with smartphones to track their activities and collect data from the field. The department is therefore working on developing a system in which LHWs can use their own phones to report data from the field through SMS. The department is also considering the possibility of using SIMs to keep track of where the workers are when they send data. The accuracy of tracking the SIM remains problematic, however.

Leave Management

Automating the process of submitting, and obtaining approval for, a leave request could help differentiate legitimate and illegitimate absences. An employee may request leave through SMS and receive approval the same way. Using this system would allow leave information for each employee to be collected in an online dashboard that can track every employee's leaves and manage them fairly. It could potentially be a game changer in managing school attendance, as leave information could be actively monitored and incentives for teachers could be calibrated on the basis of the data (figure A.7).

Attendance Monitoring

Most field worker activity monitoring systems are based on maintaining paper attendance registers. Because they are easy to forge, such manual systems deliver unreliable data and are insufficient to deter absenteeism. However, proof of presence on a particular day can be collected reliably using smartphones with cameras. To record attendance, a group photo of all the staff present at a school or health unit can be taken with a

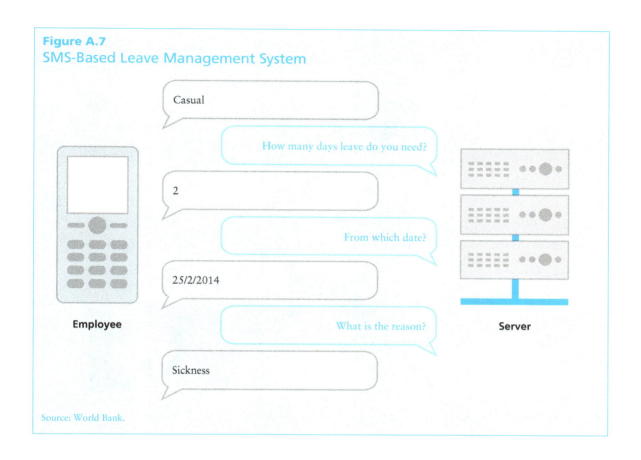

Figure A.7
SMS-Based Leave Management System

Casual

How many days leave do you need?

2

From which date?

25/2/2014

What is the reason?

Sickness

Employee

Server

Source: World Bank.

phone's built-in camera and transmitted to a central server, as shown in figure A.8.

An individual's attendance can be recorded based on face recognition software. Since each photo will have an embedded time stamp and location, the photo cannot be tampered with. Photos can be taken daily or as periodic spot checks to verify attendance records that have been collected in other ways. Depending on the degree of accuracy needed, human or automated auditing, or a combination, can be used.

Infrastructure Monitoring

The development of infrastructure is often difficult to monitor if field officers fail to visit sites regularly. Smartphones can be helpful here. The monitoring officers can be required to geo-tag their data entries and take photos to prove their presence. Even better, they can geo-tag

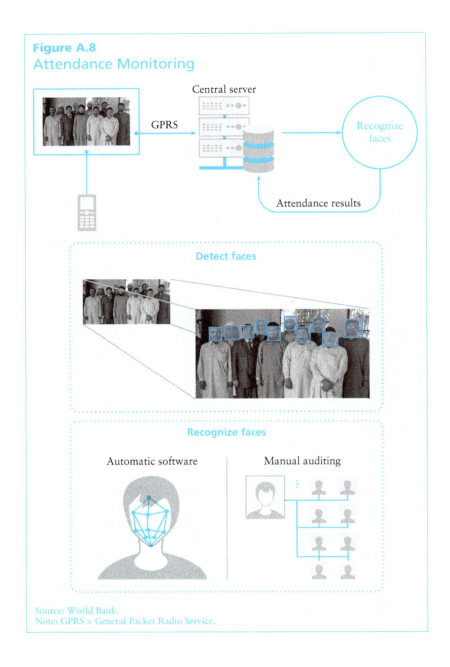

Figure A.8
Attendance Monitoring

Source: World Bank.
Note: GPRS = General Packet Radio Service.

the location of development projects using the phones or take photos of the stages of construction to avoid duplication and also check visual aspects of quality.

Logging Field Movement

Field workers are often given a daily allowance to cover their travel and fuel costs. The allowance, called a POL allowance in Punjab, for "petroleum, oil, and lubricants," is determined based on a flat rate for each day spent in the field. The system can result in unfair or inaccurate distribution of allowances because workers cover areas of different sizes. The flat rate may result in underestimation—or more likely, overestimation—of the distance traveled. However, smartphones can be used to trace the locations where a field worker submitted data entries, so that fuel allowances can then be allocated based on actual distance traveled each day (figure A.9). Although still an approximation, it will be much more accurate than the fixed rate and will contribute to savings and prevent leakages.

Figure A.9
POL or Fuel Allowances Benchmarked to Actual Performance

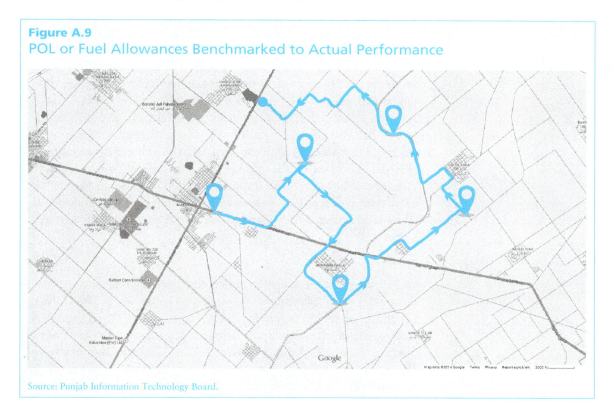

Source: Punjab Information Technology Board.

Damage Assessment

When a disaster occurs, a rugged mechanism is required to assess and document the damage and plan for aid, reconstruction, or compensation. Damage assessments are notorious for fraud, as potential beneficiaries or surveyors may misstate the extent of damage to obtain greater compensation. With Android phones, the extent of damage for each house in an affected area can be recorded using a mobile phone application, or app. Such an app was recently created for the government of Punjab by its Urban Unit, a body that assists the government in applying technology to various operations. The app records a site's spatial coordinates, along with a photo for validation. The data can then be submitted to a database directly from the phone and analyzed.

Call Center–Based Applications

Call centers are often used for help lines and as complaint receiving centers. More creative use of call centers could substantially increase their effectiveness. The Water and Sanitation Agency of Lahore (WASA) has developed a state-of-the-art complaint operation using a call center to log all complaints in a dashboard. Once a complaint is logged, an SMS is automatically sent to the appropriate officer for action. All officers of WASA can also log into the dashboard online and see all unresolved complaints at any time. Once it has resolved a complaint, the department so marks it in the dashboard. WASA has also added a functionality whereby agents call some complainants after 24 hours to verify that their complaint was indeed resolved. The data on the number of complaints, their nature, and rates of resolution are also important to allow WASA to keep track of its performance. The dashboard has several summary reports and analyses that WASA management can use to gauge the agency's performance.

Feedback

Calling is an excellent way to collect feedback from clients, especially those who are not literate or not equipped to use SMS. The Citizen Feedback model in Punjab, for example, relies on SMS to solicit feedback from citizens who have used a government service. They are queried about the quality of service delivery and whether they were asked for bribes. Figure A.10 shows a page in the Citizen Feedback model dashboard, with the data collected by call agents.

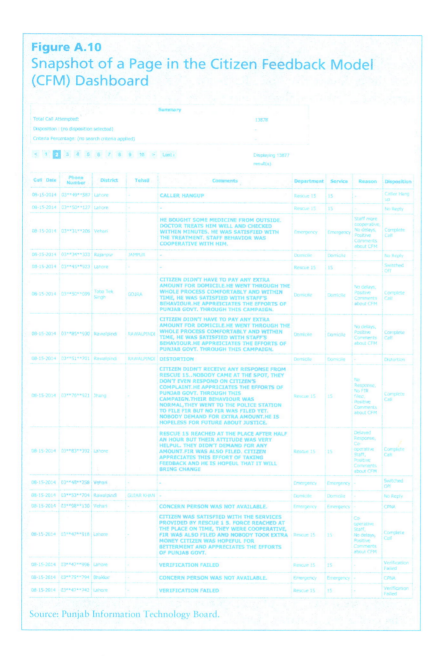

Figure A.10

Snapshot of a Page in the Citizen Feedback Model (CFM) Dashboard

Source: Punjab Information Technology Board.

Information Dissemination

When SMS is not a good medium to disseminate information, robocalls or Interactive Voice Response (IVR) methods are good alternatives. Calls are slightly more expensive than SMS but are extremely useful in reaching people who cannot use text. Robocalls are able to convey information quickly to a widespread audience that otherwise may not have any source of information. The Citizen Feedback Model uses robocalls to inform citizens that they are about to receive a text message and to ask for their feedback. The call alerts the citizen that if he or she is unable to read or respond to the SMS feedback solicitation, they should seek help from someone else to reply to the inquiry.

If a more customized method than robocalls is required, then IVR might be a better choice. With IVR, the user may call a number to collect information on a particular topic. The IVR call offers a menu with a range of options. The listener can choose the most suitable one. Private companies such as airlines or customer help lines commonly use menus to relay to customers answers to frequently asked questions. Such dissemination tools can be modified to deliver weather information, market prices to farmers, or service fees and procedural information for government services. IVR or robocall information dissemination tools are also implemented most conveniently through call centers.

Dashboards Make Smart Proactive Government Work

Collecting quality monitoring and feedback data is the first step of the smart proactive government. Analyzing the data, communicating the information to different tiers of management, and conveying feedback information to employees and the public are of equal significance. In 2002, Shirley Franklin was elected mayor of Atlanta, at a time when government systems were reputed to have minimal transparency and citizen trust in government competency was low. Mayor Franklin recognized that the fundamental problem in the existing system was lack of performance data, which reinforced the lack of a performance culture. Franklin's administration recognized the dire need for a performance metric—a system to provide accurate and timely information about the state of city services. They wanted to provide a public window into the city's operating environment, to increase transparency and ultimately citizen trust in the government (Edwards and Thomas 2005). Thus the Atlanta Dashboard was born. That is the nickname given to the performance measurement system that Mayor Franklin introduced. It served to communicate data on both the quality (through citizen feedback) and the quantity (predefined indicators) of service delivery, to enable the government to improve the efficiency of service delivery and also to increase transparency through communication with the public.

Box A.1 highlights a key aspect of the Atlanta Dashboard, the importance of evaluating performance by assessing not only quantity indicators, but also citizen perceptions of quality.

The Dashboard's Potential to Close the Loop

What happens after information is displayed on the dashboard? Initially the availability of information may motivate employees and the government to perform. But the real challenge is to make the pressure sustainable. How do we ensure (a) that employees know they are always being held accountable; (b) that citizens trust the government and believe their feedback is being acted upon; (c) that pressure on the government to perform is maintained; and (d) that senior officials can obtain quick responses on issues that are spotted on the dashboard? In essence, how do we ensure that providing real-time access to quality monitoring and feedback data actually improves transparency, accountability, and ultimately service delivery?

We believe that the answer to those questions lies in "closing the feedback loop," that is, leveraging the information on the dashboard for follow-up communication. Inflow of information to the dashboard provides the initial impetus, but it is the subsequent, outward communication to employees and the public that will generate enhanced accountability, transparency, and citizen trust. The following are examples of the kinds of outward communication that could take place:

Automated performance-based feedback to employees. The dashboard could have features that can generate SMS messages to the best and worst performers, or any other category of workers, as recorded on the dashboard. Employees also could be ranked and their rankings shared with them through SMS generated by the dashboard. Creating competition through such nonmonetary

Box A.1
The Atlanta Dashboard

The city government of Atlanta recognized that in contrast to the private sector, the public sector lacked performance metrics to gauge customer satisfaction and simply relied on the "squeakiest wheel gets the grease" approach to customer satisfaction—if you complain enough, you get attention. That generally leads to serious misallocation of resources and government attention.

Mayor Shirley Franklin decided to take a more rigorous approach, carrying out a Citizen Satisfaction Survey every quarter, with questions such as, Are the streets clean? Do you feel safe in your neighborhood? and Are there enough parks? The idea was to add the results from the survey to other operating measures in city departments. Thus the police would be responsible not only for reducing the number of burglaries, but also for ensuring that people feel safe. The public works commissioner is responsible not only for filling potholes, but also for ensuring that people feel that the roads are in good condition.

This may not sound like a noteworthy innovation, but it represented a huge change in the way the city of Atlanta was governed. As Edwards and Thomas (2005) wrote,

> Being held accountable for citizens' perceptions is very different from being held accountable for executing a business process. Departmental managers now have to reconsider the mix of services they are providing, how they should cooperate with third parties to maximize the impact of their own efforts, and how they should market their services. If the Department of Public Works is being measured simply by the miles of streets it resurfaces, then who cares? The managers resurfaced the street; it's not their fault that someone tore it up. However, if the department is held accountable for how citizens perceive the quality of streets, then managers have a strong incentive to coordinate their efforts with local companies to ensure the city's repaving schedule does not conflict with other street-related construction. Outputs such as sweeping streets and fixing sidewalks are what a city does, but those outputs are only useful if they improve citizens' quality of life. We decided that the only way to know for sure whether those outputs are leading to the right outcomes is to ask citizens.

Source: Edwards and Thomas 2005.

incentives is likely to produce a positive impact on performance. Moreover, communicating constant feedback on performance will facilitate a performance culture that will build accountability into the system.

Allowing wide access to the dashboard. Making the dashboard accessible not only to senior officials, but also to staff and the general public has the potential to increase both transparency and accountability. All the information being collected needs to be visible to the broader citizenry, so that they know what is happening. Social media could also play a role, allowing information to be broadcast to citizens in multiple forums. That will not only build the credibility and transparency of the government, but also become a source of pressure for the government to resolve problems with service delivery. It will ensure that higher managers sustain pressure on field staff to comply. Regular performance feedback to employees through the dashboard is also likely to create pressure for them to improve performance. In one case, simply highlighting underperforming facilities in red on the dashboard improved response by upper management as well as from the field (Callen et al. 2013). That they were seen as "red" facilities had a significant psychological effect, spurring workers to improve performance.

Rapid monitoring through a question-and-answer chat space. The dashboard could have a chat room that allows senior officials to acquire quick feedback on any problem through an automated SMS system built into the dashboard. The senior official can pose a question to a certain employee about a problem highlighted on the dashboard. The question goes to that employee by SMS via a built-in trigger in the dashboard. The employee's response (also via SMS) is then captured on the dashboard chat space, which can be viewed by the senior official. This would enable quick action on monitoring data. It would also speed up the monitoring action cycle by moving it from paper or e-mail communication to SMS communication.

Trust for citizens and rents for politicians through broad-based communication. Any government action based on citizen feedback displayed on the dashboard also could be broadcast via SMS or robocalls. That would build citizen trust in the government and also ensure that the quality of citizen feedback improves progressively. Moreover, given that government action is likely to be in areas where citizens demand change, broadcasting the changes will also create political rents for politicians and thus align their political incentives with better performance.

Design Principles and Implementation

In his book *Information Dashboard Design* (2013), Stephen Few proposes four steps that are essential to consider in designing a dashboard for any performance monitoring process: Make the manager aware of the situation at a broad level; identify areas that need attention; gather information to determine appropriate action; and take action. The four steps are the broad objectives that must be kept in mind at each stage of developing the dashboard. At each step, the following key principles should be considered:

Relevance. Reports should revolve around key pieces of information that are relevant to the problem identified by the manager. They should allow the manager to assess performance of his staff and take action based on the information presented, whether targets, achievements, benchmarks, trends, or future projections.

Main landing page. The most important view is the first landing page that users see when they open the dashboard. The main page content must be carefully formatted because the user will work from the main screen the majority of the time. The higher the user is in the management hierarchy, the more likely it is that they will spend nearly all of the time on that one screen. Therefore, the screen should give a snapshot view of an overall situation, as well as highlight areas that require attention. Even if the page cannot directly suggest actions, at the very least it should provide an alert for the manager to lead him to a problem that needs action.

Access control and the management hierarchy. Design customized views for different tiers of management, as each tier has different primary responsibilities. For example, a landing page for a lower-level official might have more information about data entry compliance. In contrast, reports for higher-level officials might focus on more output or outcome-level indicators. Access to some reports can be restricted to particular users or administrative units.

Colors, symbols, and sizes. Use colors, symbols, and sizes to give a one-glance overview of which indicators or units (geographical units, facilities, functional units) are meeting their targets and which require attention. Appropriate colors can create an obvious contrast between what needs attention and what doesn't. Note, however, that variation in visual cues should be used sparingly and only when the user needs to be alerted.

Minimize scrolling. Fit as much as possible onto one screen, particularly for the first page or so, as that is where the user spends the most time. Doing this is challenging because it requires knowing exactly what the user needs to see, for example, absolute numbers, trends, or comparisons to targets. More often than not, there will be too much information to fit into one screen, and it will have to be segmented. Decide how it should be segmented based on how each user will look at the data. Segmentation could be done on spatial units or on type of indicator.

Quality of data. Dashboards, like any other automated system, require data to be received in a consistent format. Data collection and compilation protocols must therefore be predetermined and the format strictly followed to ensure quality data. That is essential if meaningful reports are to be extracted; insufficient or poor quality data will skew results or make it difficult to identify trends.

Benchmarking and situation awareness. Absolute numbers rarely mean much on their own. They need to be compared against something to show good or bad performance. For every graph, table, or other visualization, always give a context, such as previous months, other cities or administrative units for the same month, average numbers, targets, and so forth.

Users. Know what the users are accustomed to seeing and what their regular workflow was before the introduction of technology. In organizations where ICT is not common, managers are used to seeing data in tabular form and on paper. Include tabular views in the dashboard and make screens printable. If the dashboard will be used during meetings and displayed in a projection, the visuals and resolution should be adjusted accordingly. Reduce the gap in familiarity with the technology, so as to reduce resistance and increase uptake and acceptance.

Practical Examples of Dashboards

Whether for SMS, smartphone, or call center–based data collection, setting up a dashboard that is easy to use and can present the collected data effectively is the last and one of the most crucial steps of the overall data collection process. Figures A.11, A.12, and A.13 show sample dashboard views.

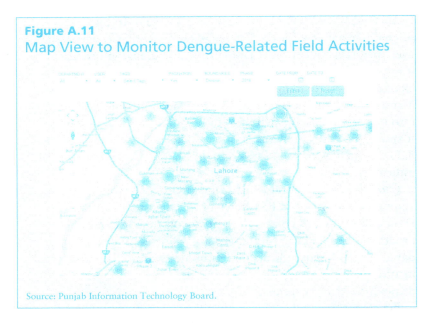

Figure A.11
Map View to Monitor Dengue-Related Field Activities

Source: Punjab Information Technology Board.

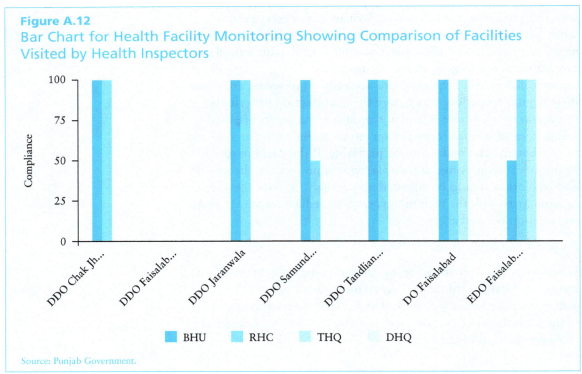

Figure A.12
Bar Chart for Health Facility Monitoring Showing Comparison of Facilities Visited by Health Inspectors

Source: Punjab Government.

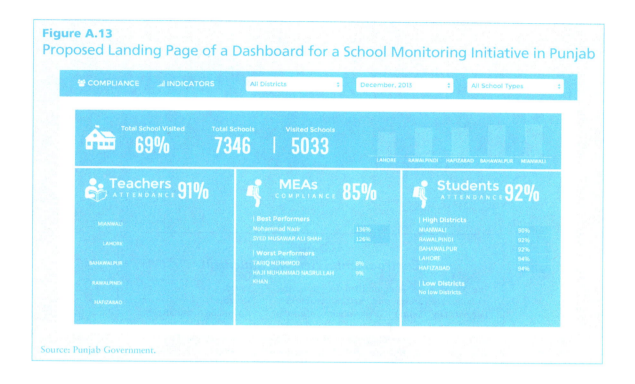

Figure A.13

Proposed Landing Page of a Dashboard for a School Monitoring Initiative in Punjab

Source: Punjab Government.

References

Callen, Michael Joseph, Saad Gulzar, Ali Hasanain, and Muhammad Yasir Khan. 2013. "The Political Economy of Public Employee Absence: Experimental Evidence from Pakistan." August 26. Available at Social Science Research Network, http://ssrn.com/abstract=2316245, or http://dx.doi.org/10.2139/ssrn.2316245.

Edwards, David, and John Clayton Thomas. 2005. "Developing a Municipal Performance-Measurement System: Reflections on the Atlanta Dashboard." *Public Administration Review* 65 (3): 369–76.

Few, Stephen. 2013. *Information Dashboard Design: Displaying Data for At-a-Glance Monitoring.* 2d ed. Oakland, CA: Analytics Press.

Trucano, Michael. 2013. "Ten Principles to Consider When Introducing ICTs into Remote, Low-Income Educational Environments" (blog). https://blogs.worldbank.org/edutech/10-principles-consider-when-introducing-icts-remote-low-income-educational-environments.

ECO-AUDIT
Environmental Benefits Statement

The World Bank is committed to preserving endangered forests and natural resources. ***Logged On: Smart Government Solutions from South Asia*** was printed on recycled paper with 30 percent postconsumer fiber in accordance with the recommended standards for paper usage set by the Green Press Initiative, a nonprofit program supporting publishers in using fiber that is not sourced from endangered forests. For more information, visit www.greenpressinitiative.org.

Saved:
- 4 trees
- 2 million British thermal units of total energy
- 363 pounds of net greenhouse gases (CO_2 equivalent)
- 1,969 gallons of waste water
- 132 pounds of solid waste

www.ingramcontent.com/pod-product-compliance
Lightning Source LLC
Chambersburg PA
CBHW080422060326
40689CB00019B/4341